Between Ideology and
Realpolitik

Recent Titles in
Contributions to the Study of World History

Between Ideology and *Realpolitik*

*Woodrow Wilson and the
Russian Revolution, 1917–1921*

GEORG SCHILD

Contributions to the Study of World History, Number 51

GREENWOOD PRESS
WESTPORT, CONNECTICUT • LONDON

Library of Congress Cataloging-in-Publication Data

Schild, Georg
    Between ideology and *realpolitik* : Woodrow Wilson and the Russian
Revolution, 1917-1921 / Georg Schild.
       p.   cm.—(Contributions to the study of world history, ISSN
0885-9159 ; no. 51)
    Includes bibliographical references and index.
    ISBN 0-313-29570-0 (alk. paper)
    1. United States—Foreign relations—Soviet Union. 2. Soviet
Union—Foreign relations—United States. 3. Soviet Union—History—
Revolution, 1917-1921—Diplomatic history. 4. Wilson, Woodrow,
1856-1924. I. Title. II. Series.
E183.8.S65S35   1995
327.7304'09'091—dc20   94-46927

British Library Cataloguing in Publication Data is available.

Library of Congress Catalog Card Number: 94-46927
ISBN: 0-313-29570-0
ISSN: 0885-9159

First published in 1995

Greenwood Press, 88 Post Road West, Westport, CT 06881
An imprint of Greenwood Publishing Group, Inc.

Printed in the United States of America

The paper used in this book complies with the
Permanent Paper Standard issued by the National
Information Standards Organization (Z39.48-1984).

10 9 8 7 6 5 4 3 2 1

Wilson's historic achievement lies in his recognition that Americans cannot sustain major international engagements that are not justified by their moral faith. His downfall was in treating the tragedies of history as aberrations, or as due to the shortsightedness and the evil of individual leaders, and in his rejection of any objective basis for peace other than the force of public opinion and the worldwide spread of democratic institutions.

— Henry Kissinger, *Diplomacy*, p. 50

Contents

Abbreviations

FRUS	United States, Department of State, *Papers Relating to the Foreign Relations of the United States*
LC	Library of Congress, Washington, D.C.
NA	National Archives, Washington, D.C.
PPWW	Ray S. Baker, ed., *The Public Papers of Woodrow Wilson*
PWW	Arthur S. Link, ed., *The Papers of Woodrow Wilson*
RPG	Robert Browder, Alexander Kerensky, eds., *The Russian Provisional Government*

Introduction

In one of his last public statements before his death, Woodrow Wilson returned to a problem that had concerned him throughout his second term as president of the United States: the Russian Revolution of 1917. In an article for the August 1923 issue of *The Atlantic Monthly*, he attempted to explain the origins of that revolution six years earlier. Wilson interpreted it as a result of certain "defects" in the Russian political and social system during the time of tsarism:

What gave rise to the Russian Revolution? The answer can only be that it was the product of a whole social system. . . . It was due to the systematic denial to the great body of Russians of the rights and privileges which all normal men desire. . . . The lives of the great mass of the Russian people contained no opportunities, but were hemmed in by barriers against which they were constantly flinging their spirits. . . . It has to be noted as a leading fact in our time that it was against "capitalism" that the Russian leaders directed their attacks.[1]

Wilson went on to justify a revolt against certain forms of unlimited capitalism: "Is it not . . . true that the capitalists have often seemed to regard the men whom they used as mere instruments of profit, whose physical and mental powers it was legitimate to exploit with as slight cost to themselves as possible, either of money or of sympathy?" Wilson referred not only to Russian capitalism, but also to capitalism and exploitation in general. If revolutions were the consequences of defective social systems, the best way to avoid them was to abandon unjust, un-Christian, and immoral behavior. Wilson sketched the outlines of a positive, antirevolutionary social system that stressed "sympathy and help-fulness and a willingness to forego self-interest in order to promote the welfare, happiness, and contentment of others and the commu-nity as a whole."[2]

Wilson proposed that a sense of community should replace the predominant individualism that could be observed not only in Russia, but also in the United States. The Russian Revolution served as an occasion for him to express his warnings to the American people. The events in Petrograd in November 1917 exemplified a political development that had to be prevented in the United States. He warned that "democracy has not yet made the world safe against irrational revolution." That "supreme task, which is nothing less than salvation of civilization, now faces democracy, insistent, imperative."[3]

Wilson's image of the Russian revolution as portrayed in 1923 was contradictory. He first called the Bolshevik coup d'état the result of an exploitative social system, then an irrational and unforeseeable event. The socialist revolutionaries of 1917 were both the victims of tsarist oppression and the followers of a political theory that Wilson despised—socialism in the Russian form of Bolshevism. Socialist ideas of public ownership of the means of production, party domination instead of democracy, and, above all, atheism, were anathema to Wilson's personal convictions.[4] The ambivalent judgment about the Bolshevik revolution that Wilson expressed in 1923 was indicative of the difficulties he had in reacting to the events in Russia a few years earlier as president.

By the time Wilson became president in 1913, U.S. political, economic, and intellectual interests in Russia had been limited for some time and diplomatic relations with that autocratic state had been cool. Those Americans who showed an interest in Russian affairs, liberals and Russian emigrés, criticized the government of the tsars and the recurring persecutions of all who were not orthodox Christians, particularly Jews, since the late nineteenth century. When the Imperial Russian government's continued com-mercial discrimination against former Russian Jews who had emigrated to America became a public issue in the United States in 1911, the House of Representatives voted to abrogate the Russian-American Commercial Treaty of 1832. As a result, economic relations, too, remained limited until Russian purchases in the United States increased after the outbreak of World War I. Americans in general, including Wilson, had only a limited interest in and understanding of Russian history or current political affairs when, during the First World War, the United States was suddenly confronted with major political upheavals there.[5]

As a direct consequence of the political ineptitude of Tsar Nicholas II and his military leadership in World War I, a group of liberal and conservative members of the Russian parliament, the Duma, forced the monarch's abdication in March of 1917 and created the so-called Provisional Government.[6] In Washington, President Wilson welcomed the revolution and granted the new Russian government immediate diplomatic recognition. In a speech before Congress in early April, Wilson called the revolution the fulfillment of the centuries-long struggle of the Russian people for democracy. In the same speech, the president also requested a congressional declaration of war against Germany. The United States entered the First World War in the spring of 1917 on the side of England, France, and the new democratic Russia.[7]

The Provisional Government, however, was plagued from the start by strong domestic opposition and by the continuing war. Popular support for the new government eroded over the summer because of its resistance to implementing a land reform and its refusal to call for an immediate ending of the war. In November 1917, only eight months after the democratic revolution, the radical socialist Bolshevik party under the leadership of Vladimir Il'ich Lenin, overthrew the Provisional Government in a *coup d'état*. In contrast to the Provisional Government, the Bolsheviks promised to conclude an immediate peace and to redistribute the farmland to those who worked it. The Bolsheviks proclaimed themselves the avant-garde for future socialist revolutions in other countries, namely, in Germany, England, and France. Leon Trotsky, one of the leading theoreticians of socialist revolutions, believed that the First World War had "transformed the whole of Europe into a powder magazine of social revolution. The Russian proletariat is now throwing a flaming torch into that powder magazine." Many West European observers agreed with that view. Walther Rathenau, a

German industrialist, who would become foreign minister during the Weimar Republic, observed in 1919 that the war "had been destined to develop into a world revolution." The First World War became the catalyst that enabled radical socialist revolutionaries to take over power in Russia and to spread their propaganda into the war-devastated states of Western and Central Europe and even into the United States.[8]

President Wilson's statements about Bolshevism after November 1917 demonstrated his constant efforts to comprehend that phenomenon. His assertions alternated between an outright condemnation of Bolshevism and an acknowledgment of the validity of certain Soviet complaints. For the president, Bolshevism had two distinct sides. In theory, it was a justifiable protest against the economic inequality in the world. In practical terms, however, it went beyond being a remedy and created new, more serious, grievances. "My heart is with them, but my mind has a contempt for them," Wilson declared of the Bolsheviks in November 1917, shortly after their revolution. In January 1919, dissatisfied with unsuccessful British and French attempts to topple the Soviet government, he told the delegates to the Paris Peace Conference that "there was certainly a latent force behind Bolshevism which attracted as much sympathy as its more brutal aspects aroused general disgust. There was throughout the world a feeling of revolt against the large vested interests which influenced the world both in the economic and political sphere." The way to "cure this domination," Wilson explained, was "constant discussion and a slow process of reform." Bolshevik ideology, he went on, was designed to eradicate the social injustices that stemmed from an adversarial relationship between capital and labor. "The seeds of Bolshevism could not flourish without a soil ready to receive them. If this soil did not exist, Bolshevism could be neglected." As the best way to contain Bolshevism, Wilson recommended that the Western democratic states should eradicate its causes, such as economic hardships of large segments of the population.[9]

Wilson's uncertainty about the true nature of Bolshevism evolved into a complex and to a certain degree contradictory policy toward Soviet Russia. In the weeks following the October Revolution, he often drew a connection between the interests of the Bolsheviks and those of Imperial Germany, and he consistently refused granting the Soviet government diplomatic recognition. But

Wilson also did not grant recognition to any of the localized anti-Bolshevik resistance groups in Russia. Until mid-1919, he even refused to provide antirevolutionary "White" groups with material aid, and he only changed his mind under considerable pressure from the British and French governments.

In contrast to the U.S. administration, the governments in London and Paris followed an openly hostile policy toward the Bolsheviks. As early as December 1917, British and French foreign and war department officials discussed plans for an invasion of Russia with the goal of overthrowing the Bolsheviks. They tried to convince the United States to join their effort. Wilson's decisions concerning Soviet Russia, therefore, also have to be seen against the background of unity among the Western democracies during the First World War and during the Paris Peace Conference.[10]

The confrontation between Wilson and Lenin after November 1917 was the first clash between liberal democracy and socialism and marked the beginning of the conflict between the two ideologies that would continue to vie for global influence throughout most of the twentieth century. Both the American president and the leader of the Soviet revolution saw the world war as a chance to spread their ideological beliefs. Wilson made it clear after the American entry into the war that the United States fought against German autocracy for liberal democracy and for the creation of an international security organization, the League of Nations. Lenin believed that the proletariat of Western Europe would rise against its oppressors and establish a socialist order once it realized the true exploitative goals of its capitalist governments.

Wilson's ideological convictions were rooted in his religious beliefs and in his faith in the superiority of democracy over all other forms of government. The United States, as the country that embodied Christianity, democracy, and liberal capitalism, possessed a superior moral and political position. As Wilson put it in 1912: "I believe that God presided over the inception of this nation . . . [w]e are chosen, and prominently chosen, to show the way to the other nations of the world how they shall walk in the paths of liberty." Wilson's view of America's mission in the world, as described by the president's biographer Arthur S. Link, was not to attain wealth and power, but to serve humankind through leadership in moral purposes.[11]

Throughout his academic and political life, Wilson interpreted political relations between Europe and the United States as a dichotomy between the traditional Old World and the superior New World that had shed the petty nationalistic rivalries that caused recurring wars in Europe. The American entry into the First World War, however, temporarily broke that tradition. In 1917 and 1918, the United States sided with one group of European states against another. Historians of the Wilson administration have long focused on the president's efforts to remain ideologically untainted despite his dealings with the British, French, and Italian governments during the First World War. The Wilsonian problem, as historian N. Gordon Levin put it in his study *Woodrow Wilson and World Politics*, was "how to be *in* but yet not completely *of* the existing international political system."[12]

During the First World War, Wilson became more intimately involved in the existing international political system than he had ever intended. Despite his continued belief in the superiority of liberal democracy and American moral values, Wilson complied with many controversial Allied demands throughout the war years. Foremost among those demands was the dispatch of U.S. troops to intervene in the Russian civil war. Wilson had initially considered such an intervention to be a violation of his liberal principles, but was finally persuaded to follow the British and French lead.

Ideological preconceptions played an important part in Wilson's grand foreign political schemes, such as the creation of the League of Nations, his fight for the approval of the Treaty of Versailles in the United States Senate, and his expectations of an eventual victory of the democratic forces in the Russian civil war. It is an altogether different question what role ideological considerations played in his day-to-day foreign political decisions. Contemporary critics of the president charged that sometimes he merely used moral arguments to justify political decisions that were based on other considerations. Randolph S. Bourne, for example, an opponent of the American entry into the First World War, noted that Wilson changed his rhetoric after 1917 and started depicting the war as a struggle for Allied survival in Europe. If the Central Powers posed such a threat to the United States and Western European democracies, it was incomprehensible that the president had not responded to that threat earlier than April 1917, but had maintained a strict neutrality for almost three years.[13]

This study of U.S. policy toward Soviet Russia of the years 1917 through 1921 concludes that the role of ideological preconceptions in Wilson's (and also in Lenin's) policymaking was more complex than historians have so far assumed. Political, economic, and military necessities dictated that some of the most important American (and Soviet) foreign policy decisions of the years 1917 through 1919 were based on considerations of *realpolitik* rather than ideology. Lenin, for example, accepted the humiliating treaty of Brest-Litovsk in the winter of 1917/18 instead of calling for a revolutionary war in Germany as many other leading Bolsheviks demanded at the time. Lenin felt forced to do so because revolutionary expectations had not materialized in Germany and the remnants of the Russian army were no match for the Imperial German *Reichswehr*. Two years later, in the spring of 1920, Lenin appealed to Russian nationalism, as opposed to proletarian internationalism, when Polish armies under Marshal Joseph Pilsudski occupied the Ukraine. Similarly, Wilson's decisions to enter the First World War and his agreement in the summer of 1918 to intervene in the Russian civil war stood in contrast to his initial decisions to remain neutral in the war and to refrain from intervening in Russia and can therefore not be attributed to his Christian and liberal democratic philosophy. Instead, the president felt compelled to change his mind because of the need to maintain a viable Eastern front for defeating the economic competition and military threat of Imperial Germany and for promoting alliance cohesion in the First World War. After the end of the war, the president returned to a more purely ideological foreign policy when he subordinated his Russian policy to expectations of an imminent democratization of Soviet Russia.

While Wilson used ideological and moralistic rhetoric to justify all important decisions, he sometimes compromised his ideological convictions to suit other interests. In the fight for approval of the Treaty of Versailles, Wilson did not allow any compromise with reluctant senators. Instead, he ruined his own health in his effort to convince the American people that he alone was correct on that question. In other instances, however, particularly the entry into the First World War and the intervention in Russia, he displayed a considerable willingness to compromise with the British and French views. Moral arguments in those two areas, therefore, have to be seen as merely indicating strong convictions, but not necessarily a reference as to what triggered the political decision. Wilson's Russian policy, in other words, was conceived in a frame between ideology and *realpolitik*.

1

War and Revolution

There are those today who see the winter of 1917–1918 as one of the great turning points of modern history, the point at which there separated and branched out, clearly and for all to see, the two great conflicting answers—totalitarian and liberal—to the emerging problems of the modern age: populousness, individualism, urbanism. . . . The one concept was indeed personified, and sharply defined, by Lenin; the other, dimly and less adequately, by Wilson.

— George F. Kennan, *The Decision to Intervene*[1]

On 2 April 1917, President Woodrow Wilson appeared before a joint session of the United States Congress and asked for a declaration of war against Imperial Germany. As the reason for his request, he cited the German decision of January to conduct unrestricted submarine warfare in the waters off Great Britain. The submarines would wage a war against all nations, including the United States: "American ships have been sunk, American lives taken." With its attacks, Germany would violate American rights to trade as a neutral. The right, Wilson said, "is more precious than peace, and we shall fight for the things which we have always carried nearest our hearts,—for democracy, . . . for the rights and liberties of small nations, for a universal dominion of right by such a concert of free peoples as shall bring peace and safety to all nations and make the world itself at last free." On 4 April, the Senate passed the War Resolution with 82 to 6 votes; two days later, the House of Representatives followed suit with a 373 to 50 vote; President Wilson signed it the same day.[2]

In April 1917, the United States entered a war that had been going on in Europe for almost three years. In his initial reaction to the outbreak of the conflict in the summer of 1914, President Wilson had urged the American people to remain neutral in the war. Aided by his closest personal friend and adviser Colonel Edward M. House and by Secretary of State William Jennings Bryan, Wilson tried to mediate between the belligerents as his predecessor, Theodore Roosevelt, had done during the Russo-Japanese War in 1905. It soon became obvious, however, that Wilson and Bryan held different views about the rights of neutrals during wars and about the larger implications of the European war for the United States. Avoiding an American military involvement in Europe was the ultimate goal of Bryan's foreign policy, and he was willing to subordinate American rights as a neutral to that predominant aim. Wilson, in contrast, insisted on the American right as a neutral country to trade with belligerents in noncontraband commodities, but he was unsure about how far he should go in defending those rights. After German submarines torpedoed the British liner *Lusitania* in May 1915, killing 1,200 passengers, among them 128 Americans, Bryan suggested issuing only a mild protest and warning Americans not to travel on ships of belligerents. Wilson disagreed with his secretary of state and insisted in a note to the German government that Americans had the right to travel on belligerent ships through war zones. When the government in Berlin reacted evasively to the note, Bryan feared that Wilson's continued insistence on the rights of neutrals would bring the United States closer to war and on 8 June resigned from his post. Shortly thereafter Wilson sent a second, more strongly worded note to Berlin. But the president was not prepared to go to war over the *Lusitania* incident. For the next two years, Wilson's foreign policy statements alternated between calls for greater American involvement in the conflict and quasi-isolationist statements.[3]

After Bryan's resignation, Wilson nominated Robert Lansing, an international lawyer and State Department counselor, as the new

secretary of state. Lansing's views on the war and its implications
for the United States differed greatly from his predecessor's and
initially also from the president's. Lansing believed that a victory
of the Central Powers in the war would lead to German hegemony
in Europe and to German interference in the Western Hemisphere.
The new secretary became an early advocate of American entry
into the war on the side of the Entente because he considered an
Allied victory necessary for the security of the United States.
Lansing even undermined Wilson's attempt to mediate peace in
December 1916 out of fear that a mediation effort might jeopardize
an Allied victory. After the president had sent peace notes to the
governments at war, Lansing told journalists that neither the
president nor he regarded the documents as peace notes. Wilson's
secretary publicly raised doubts about the validity of a presidential
initiative. If Lansing was right in his statement, he had publicly
embarrassed the president; if he was wrong, he had potentially
sabotaged a major American peace initiative.[4]

While his assessment of the dangers of the European war for the
United States compelled Lansing to advocate an American entry
into the conflict on the British side, Wilson rejected that view for
ideological reasons. As late as October 1916, he asked his audience
during a campaign rally in Cincinnati whether they had ever heard
what had started the European war. "If you have," he told his
listeners, "I wish you would publish it, because nobody else has.
So far as I can gather, nothing in particular started it, but everything
in general." Wilson diagnosed a "mutual suspicion" that had grown
in Europe, a "complex web of intrigue and spying." In his interpretation of the above passage, historian N. Gordon Levin points out
that Wilson's speech remained within the ideological pattern of
liberal anti-imperialism and American exceptionalism. More important, however, was the fact that his ideological interpretation
led Wilson not to support the Allies, but to reject the validity of
either side's war efforts. He refused to distinguish between one
good and one bad party more than two years into the war. Only
half a year later, however, Wilson asked for a decision of war against
Germany. Levin believed that both Wilson's initial rejection of all
European war efforts and his later joining the war on the side of
the Allies were based on "certain latent ideological tendencies
which would help motivate an American liberal war against Germany." A different interpretation is that a realist thinking along the

lines of Secretary Lansing slowly gained the upper hand in the White House in 1916 and 1917. Economic and security considerations appeared to be the most important factor in determining Wilson's decision to enter the war.[5]

Wilson continued his remarks in Cincinnati by pointing out the general threat of wars to the security of the United States. The current war was the last one the United States could keep out of. The "business of neutrality," he declared, was over. Wars had reached such a scale that the position of neutrals had become intolerable. Again, Wilson distinguished between the United States and Europe. If America would abstain from European affairs, the old continent would continuously repeat the cycle of war.[6]

Shortly after he had proclaimed all but the end of American neutrality, Wilson again retreated and made another effort to mediate peace in Europe. On 18 December 1916, he urged the belligerents to state their war aims publicly. The note to the warring states read:

He [the president] takes the liberty of calling attention to the fact that the objects which the statesmen of the belligerents on both sides have in mind in this war are virtually the same, as stated in general terms to their own people and to the world. Each side desires to make the rights and privileges of weak peoples . . . as secure against aggression . . . as the rights . . . of the great and powerful states now at war.[7]

Wilson still did not publicly distinguish between the war aims of the Allies and the Central Powers. Instead, he insisted that their war aims appeared to be virtually identical. He hoped that he could use their responses to his appeal as a basis for another effort to mediate in the conflict. His goal, he wrote, was to end the war soon, so that "millions upon millions of lives will not continue to be sacrificed." In a speech before Congress one month later, on 22 January 1917, Wilson reviewed the replies he had received from the belligerents. The Central Powers, he stated, had declared their intention of meeting their antagonists and discussing peace terms. The Entente had responded "much more definitely" and had delineated, "in general terms, indeed, but with sufficient definiteness to imply details," the arrangements they considered necessary for a satisfactory settlement. "We are much nearer a definite discussion of the peace which shall end the present war," Wilson added optimistically. He then went on to describe his own views of a peace settlement. The peace had to be based on an equality of nations, freedom of the seas, and disarmament. The central feature, however, was that it had to be a "peace without victory." Victory, he explained "would mean peace forced upon a loser, a victor's terms imposed upon the vanquished."[8]

Wilson called those proposals "American principles, American policies," with a clear emphasis on "American." He attempted to use his moral influence as a neutral and disinterested outsider to convince the European states to end the conflict immediately and without waiting for one side to emerge victoriously. In his mediation efforts he tried to maintain an equal distance from both sides, refrained from blaming either party for specific war aims, and assured both the Entente and Central Powers that they could end the war undefeated. His peace initiative of the winter 1916/17 revealed his concern about the domination of Europe by any one state, about the horrors of the war, but also his lack of understanding of the issues at stake for the European states. Neither the British nor the German government pledged to end the war on Wilson's terms in early 1917. But the president remained undeterred. The "real people I was speaking to," he wrote to John P. Gavit, editor of the New York *Evening Post* one week after the speech, were neither the United States senators, nor the heads of foreign governments, but the "people of the countries now at war."[9] Wilson's moral approach to policy led him to believe that his position was so sound that the people in the war-torn states would listen to him instead of their own national leaders. How could the people in Berlin not see that he was disinterested in European border disputes and that his only goal was to end the war? It was this desire to be the conscience of the governments and the voice of the people that was challenged in the fall of 1917 when, after the October Revolution, the Bolsheviks began threatening to appeal to the people of the capitalist states by revealing their governments' true war aims.

Owing to a lack of understanding of the importance of the war to the European states, Wilson's peace initiatives of the winter 1916/17 were unsuccessful. Both sides in the war resented the president's questioning of their war aims and placing those aims on an equal footing. Wilson urged the Europeans to end a long and bloody conflict without a decision, to return to the prewar status quo, and to disregard territorial and financial settlements. The suffering on both sides would have been in vain. In early 1917, however, neither side had given up hope of winning the war. Wilson's initiatives would have robbed the winner of the fruits of its efforts. The president's mediation effort was understandable from the point of view of a politician observing the conflict from the far shores of the Atlantic Ocean. For Europeans, however, it was not acceptable.[10]

On 31 January 1917, the German ambassador to Washington, Count Johann von Bernstorff, informed the State Department that from 1 February on a naval blockade would be imposed on the British Isles. To enforce that blockade, all merchant and navy ships trying to reach or leave England would be subject to submarine attacks without prior warning. The German use of submarines in naval warfare differed from the searching of vessels as practiced by the British navy in one important aspect. Whereas the British navy confiscated deliveries to Germany and diverted trawlers to British harbors, German submarines torpedoed and sank merchant ships, usually without prior warning to the ships' crews. "England's violation of neutral rights is different from Germany's violation of the rights of humanity," Wilson had commented to Secretary Bryan shortly before his resignation in 1915.[11]

On 3 February 1917, the president announced that the United States would not bow to the German submarine threat and broke off diplomatic relations with Germany. With hindsight, there appeared to be a straight line from the breaking off of diplomatic relations with Germany to the declaration of war two months later. Wilson, however, did not see it that way. In speeches and private conversations in February and March, he called severing ties to Germany the only policy consistent with the "dignity and honor" of the United States. And he added: "We do not desire any hostile conflict with the Imperial German Government." Frank Cobb, the editor of the New York *World* and a personal friend of the president, remembered Wilson saying that as long as the United States remained outside of the conflict there was a "preponderance of neutrality, but if we joined the Allies the world would be off a peace basis and onto a war basis."[12]

In February, Wilson did not appear to be ready to intervene in the war. Instead, he still emphasized the positive role that a neutral United States could play in the conflict. It took another outside event to tip the scale of ideological reluctance and political necessity to intervene in favor of the latter. After American and British ships were torpedoed in February and March 1917, he asked the United States Congress for a declaration of war. But even then the United States did not become an Allied power. Wilson insisted that the United States was only associated with the British and French war efforts. America would at the same time be a part of the joint war but also different, untainted by selfish goals. The president understood the warning to avoid foreign entanglements contained in George Washington's farewell address as meaning to avoid being entangled in the ambitions and the national purposes of other nations. Wilson tried to allow the United States a greater role in the world while at the same time upholding the dichotomy of the Old World with its ambitions, and the New, "born a Christian nation" to exemplify, as he wrote, the "devotion to the elements of righteousness which are derived from the revelations of Holy Scripture."[13]

Wilson's decision to enter into the First World War was based on complex ideological and political decisions. He insisted on the right of American merchants to trade with any belligerent, and he considered Germany's U-boat attacks in violation of that right. Ideology and considerations of *realpolitik* merged in Wilson's mind. Selling goods to Europe was not to be primarily a source of profit, but a service to the Old World. He told the participants of the World's Salesmanship Congress in Detroit on 10 July 1916: "Lift your eyes to the horizon of business. Do not look too close at the little process with which you are concerned, but let your thoughts and your imagination run abroad throughout the whole world. And, with the inspiration of the thought that you are Americans and are meant to carry liberty and justice and the principle of humanity wherever you go, go out and sell goods that will make the world more comfortable and more happy, and convert them to the principles of America." Wilson identified ideological goals with those that produced tangible advantages for the United States.[14]

In April 1917, Wilson's views on the war and on the way to achieve a democratic peace after the end of the conflict changed. He no longer spoke of an immediate "peace without victory," but committed the United States to winning a complete military success to make the world "safe for democracy." In his war message speech on 2 April 1917, he began defining America's war aims. He stated that "the menace to peace and freedom lies in the existence of autocratic governments backed by organized force which is controlled wholly by their will, not by the will of the people." He committed the United States to continue fighting until the German autocracy was replaced by a democratic government there. A few weeks later, on 30 May 1917, he reiterated his war goals in general terms: "We did not set this government up in order that we might have a selfish and separate liberty, for we are now ready to come to your assistance and fight out upon the field of the world the cause of human liberty." In his State of the Union Address on 4 December 1917, Wilson again emphasized that the precondition to ending the war was establishing a democratic government in Germany. In a passing reference, he criticized the Soviet Russian calls for an immediate peace on the basis of the formula of "no annexations, no contributions" as being utilized by the "masters of German intrigue." That was well short of calling the Bolsheviks who had taken over power in Russia in November German agents, but clearly drew parallels between alleged Soviet and German war aims.[15]

Once the United States had entered the war, Wilson continued to use moral arguments in justifying his policy. After April 1917, however, the moral force was no longer on the side of the peace activists and disinterested neutrals, but on that of the forces fighting for liberty and democracy in the world. Despite his often repeated statements concerning liberal and democratic war aims, Wilson defined those goals only vaguely. It took the president almost one year, until early January 1918, to specify them in greater detail. And even that statement, the Fourteen Points speech, was precipitated more by the Russian October Revolution and the Soviet declarations of peace than by Wilson's desire to elaborate on his goals. The main reason for Wilson's reluctance to define war aims more specifically was that he knew that the Entente did not fight for liberal democratic goals, but for territorial aggrandizement and economic expansion. "England and France have not the same views with regard to peace that we have by any means," Wilson wrote to House in July 1917. One month later he wrote to him again: "I have not thought it wise to say more or to be more specific [in his draft reply to a peace initiative by Pope Benedict XV in August 1917] because it might provoke dissenting voices from France and Italy if I should,—if I should say, for example, that their territorial claims did not interest us." An unambiguous endorsement of liberal war aims without territorial annexations would have alienated the conservative politicians of the Entente states and would have been welcomed only by radical antiwar socialists in Western Europe and in Russia who criticized the war as imperialist and whom Wilson despised. The president resigned himself to attempting to influence the Entente at the peace conference after the war in order to convince them to abandon their imperialist aims.[16]

Wilson's initial approach to the First World War was to stay aloof from the petty European conflict over spheres of influence and colonies and thereby do justice to his high moral standards. After April 1917 his goal was to achieve a liberal-democratic peace—replacing the autocratic German regime with a democratic government—to justify America's entry into the war. To achieve victory in the war, however, Wilson had to ally himself with illiberal conservative politicians in Europe whose primary goal was an expansionist peace. At the Paris Peace Conference, Wilson alone called for an unselfish peace treaty; America's Allies fought for economic and territorial gains. Only radical left-wing parties in many European states supported Wilson's nonannexationist goals. When Wilson gave up calls for an immediate peace without victory in the spring of 1917, his new position left a void. During the summer, Russian socialist revolutionaries filled it. They assumed Wilson's old role of a disinterested party calling for the immediate end of the war and for a peace "without annexations and contributions."[17]

It is almost tragic that Wilson, as the champion of liberal democracy, considered the antiwar rhetoric of left-wing parties a menace and never counted them among his potential allies in his campaign for peace. In early July 1918, Assistant Secretary of the Treasury Oscar Crosby, who had shortly before returned from a trip to Europe, informed Wilson that the Allied governments in Europe did not take his League of Nations plans seriously. "Mr. Lloyd George has laughed at the proposed League in my presence, and M. Clemenceau has sneered at it." Crosby then went on to say that the socialist and labor parties took the idea of a League of Nations very seriously. Wilson, however, made it clear to him that he would not consider socialist parties his allies in the struggle for the League of Nations.[18]

Three weeks before the U.S. Congress voted to join the war on the side of the Entente, the centuries-old autocratic tsarist rule in Russia was overthrown and substituted by a quasi-democratic government. The "February Revolution," as it became known, however, was not the end of the political struggles in Russia. The hardships of the war increased the strength of radical groups that took over power in Russia in November 1917. The regime the revolutionaries set up, led by Vladimir I. Lenin, would determine Russian policy for the next seventy-five years.

For the Russian people, the war had begun almost three years before the United States entered the conflict. Over the summer of 1914, hostilities between the Habsburg Empire and Serbia developed into a European-wide war between Germany and the Austro-Hungarian Empire on the one hand, and Great Britain, France, Italy, and Russia on the other. Amidst an outpouring of patriotic fervor, Tsar Nicholas II proclaimed a state of war with Imperial Germany on 19 July (1 August[19]) 1914. It became clear almost immediately, however, that Russia was ill prepared for conducting a modern mechanized war. The first battles against the *Reichswehr* at Tannenberg and the Masurian Lakes ended in costly and demoralizing defeats. By the end of the first year's fall campaign, Russia had already lost 1.5 million men, many of them hard-to-replace officers. By the summer of 1915, Russian troops had been forced to cede important industrial centers in Poland, Lithuania, and Byelorussia to the enemy. The reasons for the Russian military disasters were manifold. The military leadership demonstrated great ineptitude during the 1914 summer and fall campaigns in East Prussia, allowing two armies to operate independently without any coordination of their movements. The country's poor infrastructure and its industry's inability to supply the military with sufficient war material aggravated the situation for the troops. Limited production and poor distribution facilities caused shortages of bullets and artillery shells.[20]

Nowhere in Europe did the war have more fundamental social and political effects than in Russia. Russia had entered the industrial revolution late in the nineteenth century. By 1914, a majority of Russians still lived in isolated rural areas. During the war, 15 million men, more than a third of all males of working age, workers from industrialized cities and peasants from far-away villages, were drafted into the military. Their absence from factories and farms had severe effects on the productivity of both industries. Grain production fell from 4 billion puds in 1915 to 3.3 billion puds in 1916, and 3.2 billion puds in 1917. Productivity in the iron smelting industry fell from 181 puds per worker per month in 1914 to 119 puds in 1917. Those decreases in productivity at a time when the military demanded an increasingly greater share of the total output led to deteriorating living conditions for the civilian population. Conditions were particularly bad in big cities; they reached a low point in the winter of 1916/17 when unusually cold weather caused additional hardships and further increased production and distribution problems.[21]

The initial patriotic support for the war lasted only a few months. While there were few strikes and antigovernment demonstrations in 1914, large-scale antiwar strikes and protests against the deteriorating living conditions began in the summer of 1915.[22] The tsarist Russian government was determined from the beginning to subdue all protests forcefully. When, between 23 and 27 February (8 and 12 March) 1917, large demonstrations again took place in the streets of Petrograd,[23] Tsar Nicholas II ordered General Sergei S. Khabalov, the commander of the Petrograd Military District, to use the military to dissolve all political gatherings. Initially, the military obeyed the order to disperse demonstrations; but on 27 February (12 March) a mutiny broke out among the Petrograd garrison, and soldiers disobeyed a command to fire on workers. Instead of following tsarist orders, the troops fraternized with the antigovernment demonstrators. Out of the roughly 160,000 men garrisoned in Petrograd, about half supported the mutiny while the other half remained neutral.[24]

With the refusal to obey the orders to break up antigovernment demonstrations, the entire system of autocracy, which was based on the unquestioned authority of the tsar, was undermined. The continuing demonstrations and the military's refusal to intervene led to a temporary power vacuum in Russia that was filled by members of the Russian parliament. On 27 February (12 March), liberal and conservative representatives of the Russian Duma formed the so-called Provisional Committee with the goal of taking responsibility for, as the Committee announced, "restoring national and public order."[25]

The political views of the members of the Provisional Duma Committee covered a wide political spectrum. Liberals and moderate socialists, such as Alexander F. Kerensky of the Social Revolutionary party, welcomed the revolution as the fulfillment of the political history of the Duma. Reactionaries, such as Vasily V. Shul'gin of the Nationalist party, abhorred the crowds in the street and hoped to return to the tsarist regime of law and order. Despite their diverse views, the Duma members agreed on one common goal. They wanted to prevent the revolution from going beyond establishing a liberal regime, in particular preventing a takeover of power by radical socialists. The fear that the revolution could get out of control and lead to anarchy led many former pro-tsarist military officers and policemen to support the Provisional Duma Committee.[26]

Parallel with the creation of the Duma Committee, socialist parties organized a competing political organization, the Provisional Executive Committee of the Soviet (council) of Workers' Deputies. Soviets had first emerged spontaneously during the abortive Russian Revolution of 1905 to organize factory workers. In the spring and summer of 1917, socialist parties revived that tradition and formed numerous councils in Russian cities. Until the October Revolution, the Soviets included members of all Russian socialist parties, not only the Bolsheviks. In fact, in the election for the Petrograd Soviet on 28 February (13 March) 1917, the radical socialist parties, among them the Bolsheviks, received only a minority of votes. Of the 3,000 members of the Petrograd Soviet in March 1917, a mere 40 were Bolsheviks. Moderate socialist parties dominated the Soviet until the fall. Mostly because of a radicalization of Russian politics over the summer of 1917, the Bolsheviks gained a majority position in the Soviet in the fall. After the October Revolution, they purged the Soviets of members from other parties. From the spring of 1918 on, the terms *Soviet* and *Bolshevik* become almost synonymous.[27]

In early March 1917, the Provisional Duma Committee and the Menshevik-dominated Executive Committee of the Petrograd Soviet began negotiations about the formation of a new government. In those negotiations, it became apparent that the views within the Soviet were as diverse as those within the Duma. In particular, the parties in the Soviet were not united in their position on taking over governmental responsibilities jointly with the Duma Committee. Moderate socialists advocated the creation of a coalition government composed of the Duma and the Soviet. Radical socialists, among them the Bolsheviks, rejected the coalition proposal and instead called for the establishment of a radical socialist government. The Soviet decided on 1 (14) March that it would neither cooperate with nor actively fight a bourgeois government, but would tolerate it.[28]

That decision meant that two power centers would exist in Russia, the Provisional Government and the Soviet. While the Soviet rejected participating in a nonsocialist government, it demanded guarantees for its power. The Soviet's primary power basis was the military, which was recruited mainly from workers and peasants. In Order No. 1 of 1 (14) March 1917, the Petrograd Soviet demanded, among other things, that soldiers not obey orders of the Duma's Military Commission if they conflicted with commands from the Soviet. The Soviet's goal was to ensure that the Provisional Government would not transfer pro-Soviet troops out of the capital and replace them with units loyal only to the Provisional Government.[29]

On 2 (15) March, Tsar Nicholas II abdicated; the same day Prince Georgii E. L'vov, a wealthy landowner and longtime member of the Russian Duma, became the first prime minister of the ten-member Russian Provisional Government. In theory, his government possessed nearly unlimited power. After the abdication of the tsar and the dissolution of the Duma, the Provisional Government served as both legislative and executive organ. But L'vov considered his government as only temporary. It was to be replaced by an elected executive as soon as possible. L'vov, therefore, was reluctant to initiate far-reaching social and economic changes. Nowhere was that passivity more pronounced than in his position on land reform. The Provisional Government never endorsed a redistribution of land and was soon confronted with a wave of peasant unrest in the countryside. In countless districts, peasants forced their landowners to surrender the land to them. On 8 (21) April, L'vov sided with the landowners and threatened to use the military for the reestablishment of peace and order in the countryside. In the volatile situation after the February Revolution, he failed to give the country a new direction by putting the provincial governments in the hands of pro-democratic politicians. Instead, he believed that the central government should reduce its influence on local affairs in the wake of the revolution. As a result, he contributed to the general anarchy that gripped the Russian provinces after the

February Revolution. L'vov was, as a recent historian noted, "an utter disaster as Prime Minister."[30]

The Provisional Government also conducted a conservative foreign policy. Foreign Minister Pavel N. Miliukov, a former history professor at the University of Moscow and a member of the conservative Constitutional Democratic party, informed the Allied governments on 4 (17) March 1917 that Russia would continue its war efforts and honor its treaties with the Allies: "[The government] is firmly convinced that the great exaltation which now animates the whole nation will multiply [its] forces and bring nearer the hour of the final triumph of regenerated Russia and of her glorious Allies." The Provisional Government also committed itself to continuing the expansionist tsarist war aims, in particular toward capturing the Dardanelles and Bosporus Straits, including Constantinople and Galicia.[31]

On 14 (27) March, the Petrograd Soviet publicly criticized the Provisional Government's position on the war-aims question. In an appeal, "To the Peoples of All the World," the Soviet proclaimed that it opposed the expansionist war-aims policy of Russia's "ruling classes." It appealed to the German proletariat to stop fighting because after the fall of tsarism Russia no longer posed a threat to the liberty of Europe. The Soviet, however, did not demand an immediate end to the war and did not generally refuse to fight for Russia: "We will firmly defend our own liberty against all reactionary attempts both from within and from without." In late March, an All-Russian Conference of Soviets reaffirmed that position in the peace question. The Soviets supported the Provisional Government in its attempts to exert pressure on the Allies to renounce the programs of conquest. The Soviets rejected Russian expansionism but supported a continuation of the war for the defense of democratic Russia.[32]

Conservative members of the Provisional Government rejected the Soviet position in the war-aims question. Foreign Minister Miliukov declared in a press interview on 22 March (4 April) that he considered the Soviet formula of "peace without annexations" a "German formula." He insisted that the Allied war aims "to alter the map of Europe in accordance with the ideas of [President] Woodrow Wilson" could not be considered as annexations. He gave examples of the territorial changes for which Russia and its Allies were fighting. The most important changes were the breakup of the Austro-Hungarian and Turkish empires. As part of the latter, in an effort to fight Turkish occupation of Southeastern Europe, Russia would annex Constantinople and the Straits.[33]

The Provisional Government steadfastly refused to enter into immediate separate peace negotiations with the Central Powers. In a note to the Allies on 18 April (1 May), Miliukov emphasized that Russia still felt bound by the treaties prohibiting separate peace negotiations with the enemy while the Allies fought to achieve a decisive victory. The statements of the Provisional Government "naturally cannot give any reason to think that the revolution which has taken place will lead to the weakening of Russia's role in the common struggle of the Allies." The Bolsheviks considered that note to be a retreat from the government's promise not to pursue expansionist war aims. It proved, in Lenin's words, that the Provisional Government continued the tsarist foreign policy, subscribed to the secret treaties, and was subservient to the interests of the French and British governments.[34]

In the wake of the dispute about the war aims, relations between the Provisional Government and the radical forces in the Petrograd Soviet deteriorated. At the same time, moderate socialists decided to join the Provisional Government. L'vov's second cabinet of 5 (18) May contained six socialist ministers. Alexander F. Kerensky, the new minister of defense, made it clear that he disagreed with the Bolshevik demands for immediate peace and tried to arouse a new wave of patriotism in the Russian people. The government would continue fighting on the side of the Entente.[35]

After the Russian February Revolution, it became immediately apparent that the new democracy was threatened by external and internal foes. Russia was still at war, and large segments of the population on the right and on the left openly rejected the new government. U.S. policy toward Russia in this situation had to try to achieve two goals: it had to secure Russia's further participation in the world war, and it had to support the forces of democracy.

Since late 1916, the American ambassador to Russia, David R. Francis, had sent the State Department increasingly alarming reports about the political situation in Petrograd. Francis, a St. Louis businessman and former governor of Missouri, had been head of the American mission there since April 1916. The selection of a businessman to represent the United States in wartime Russia appeared to indicate an American interest in improving trade relations with Russia and negotiating a new commercial treaty that would increase America's share in Russia's enormous wartime purchases.[36]

Although Francis only knew Russia in the state of war, he soon noticed the social and political tensions in Petrograd. In August 1916 he cabled to Washington: "I do not think there will be a revolution immediately after the close of the war; that would be premature, but if the Court Party does not adopt a more liberal policy by extending more privileges to the people and their representatives in the Duma, a revolution will take place before the lapse of even a few years." On 23 February 1917, the day the demonstrations that led to the overthrow of the tsar started, Francis wrote that the "[i]nternal conditions in Russia are so far from being satisfactory that they are almost threatening." General Khabalov had announced that the capital was under "military rule and that the law will be strictly enforced which means that if strikers assemble, they will be shot down if they fail to disperse when ordered to do so."[37]

On the day of the tsar's abdication, Francis cabled to the State Department:

This is undoubtedly a revolution, but it is the best managed revolution that has ever taken place for its magnitude. The Duma is assuming control and is exercising its authority in Petrograd with rare good judgment. . . . Upon the whole, Russia is to be congratulated in my judgment on the prospect of getting through an important change in government without bloodshed.[38]

In a further cable on 18 March, Francis welcomed the Russian events as the "most amazing revolution." Under wartime conditions, the Russian people had forced their emperor to abdicate and to end a more than one thousand year old monarchy and replace it with a constitutional assembly. What the Russians had accomplished was "the practical realization of that principle of government which we have championed and advocated, I mean government by consent of the governed." Francis suggested that the United States should grant the Provisional Government immediate diplomatic recognition: "Our recognition will have a stupendous moral effect especially if given first."[39]

In his euphoria, Francis underestimated the threats to the new government from the domestic political opposition. In his cable to the State Department, he wrote that there was "[n]o opposition to Provisional Government," and "[a]bsolute quiet prevails here and throughout Russia as far as known." Francis, unable to communicate in the Russian language, based his reports on information obtained from members of the new government. Francis wrote that the president of the Duma, Mikhail V. Rodzianko, and Foreign Minister Miliukov "both assure me that the entire army accepts the authority of the Provisional Government." Both Russian politicians were determined to continue the war and to fight any domestic resistance against it. Therefore, they tried to create the impression of a strong Russian government as the only way to secure further Allied assistance to Russia and to earn or gain diplomatic recognition for the new government.[40]

Officially, the Wilson administration welcomed the news of the February Revolution; unofficially, however, the president urged caution when he commented on the Russian events. On 28 March, the State Department informed Francis that the U.S. government was prepared to grant recognition to the Provisional Government.[41] The decision was officially announced two days later. In his speech before Congress on 2 April, Wilson celebrated the revolution as a victory of democracy over autocracy in Russia:

Russia was known by those who knew her best to have been always in fact democratic at heart, in all the vital habits of her thought, in all the intimate relationships of her people that spoke their natural instinct, their habitual attitude towards life. The autocracy that crowned the summit of her political structure, long as it had stood and terrible as was the reality of its power, was not in fact Russian in origin, character, or purpose; and now it has been shaken off and the great, generous Russian people have been added in all their naive majesty and might to the forces that are fighting for freedom in the world, for justice and for peace. Here is a fit partner for a League of Honour.[42]

Wilson applauded the revolutionary change of government in Russia. It was not only proof of the superiority of democracy over Russian authoritarianism, but it also helped the president in his efforts to join the Entente in the war. The main topic of Wilson's 2 April speech was not the Russian Revolution but the declaration of war on Germany. The February Revolution made it possible for

Wilson to join the war on the side of democratic nations fighting autocracy.

Wilson's statement of 2 April described the February Revolution as the end point of a long struggle for democracy in Russia. Nothing, however, could have been further from the truth. The speech demonstrated the president's limited knowledge of Russian problems and his boundless hope in Russian democracy at the time. Diplomat and historian George F. Kennan noted that "practically every element" of Wilson's speech in which he enthusiastically welcomed the Russian February Revolution "reflected a complete misunderstanding of the real situation in Russia. The statement did honor to Wilson's generous ideals, not to his knowledge of the outside world." Wilson tried to make the democratic-republican experiment of the United States fit the European context, including Russia. To him there was no alternative to the democratization of Russia. Wilson, however, was concerned about how the revolutionaries would handle their new power.[43]

Although they publicly welcomed the revolution, Wilson and Secretary Lansing felt uneasy about the potential military consequences of the February Revolution. Despite assurances that Russia would continue to fulfill its military obligations, Wilson was concerned about "whether the new government can and will wage war effectively against the Germans." In the 20 March cabinet meeting, the president expressed his concern that the Russians would try to conclude a separate peace with Germany because "they have won their freedom and . . . there is nothing to be gained by fighting longer." Reports from Russia from early April confirmed those suspicions: "naval conditions precarious, military not wholly satisfactory. Social circles urging peace and fears are entertained by some that army will be influenced thereby."[44]

Cables from Russia also reflected increasing political tensions in the aftermath of the revolution. On 3 and 10 April, the American consul in Petrograd, North Winship, described the general disregard for law and order in the capital that acutely threatened the survival of the new government. Winship noted that the situation in the city had taken a turn for the worse in recent days because of the workers' demands for increased wages and shorter working hours. The Petrograd Soviet, he noted, played a positive role in that conflict by warning the workers against disorganization. Even the "extremely radical socialists" had warned against excessive demands.[45]

Winship's detailed and differentiating reports, however, had little effect on the policy-making process in the State Department. There is no evidence that Wilson ever saw those reports or acted according to Winship's recommendations.[46] Secretary Lansing disregarded them when he continued to speak about a Russian conflict between the Provisional Government and, as he put it, "socialist elements." On 11 April, Lansing sent a memorandum to Wilson in which he expressed his concern about the situation in Russia. He suggested that the U.S. government should take steps to influence the political developments in that country: "I wish we could do something to prevent the socialistic element in Russia from carrying out any plan which would destroy the efficiency of the Allied powers." Lansing doubted that the socialist antiwar propaganda was of Russian origin. He suspected a secret German conspiracy with the aim of creating an antiwar mood in Russia and facilitating the conclusion of a separate peace treaty. "From despatches we have received," he wrote, the State Department had concluded that German socialists were "seeking to meet the Russian socialists, undoubtedly for the purpose of influencing them to support a separate peace between Germany and Russia."[47] In the following weeks, Wilson and Lansing based their Russian policy on the assumption that there was a cooperation between German groups and Russian socialists.[48] In early June, Basil Miles, the head of the State Department's Russian Division, submitted a memorandum to the secretary of state which was based on British intelligence information. In Miles's memorandum, the suspicion of a German-Russian conspiracy had already turned into a statement of fact: "It is common knowledge that the Germans are counting on their propaganda to bring about a separate peace with Russia."[49]

Wilson, too, became concerned about a conspiracy between German and Russian groups to bring about a separate peace. On 22 May, he sent a strongly worded note to Russian Foreign Minister Miliukov in which he reminded the Russians that the war was still one between democracy and autocracy. The goal of the German government was to preserve its power and its territorial occupations. The United States, in contrast, sought "no material profit or aggrandizement of any kind." The Allied armies fought "for the liberty, the self-government, and the undictated development of all peoples." Wilson called the German government's recent, more moderate war-aims statements a tactical maneuver to make a separate peace more acceptable to the Russian population. Germany had suggested a return to the borders of July 1914. But, Wilson explained, "it was the status quo ante of which this iniquitous war issued forth." The president insisted that the fighting had to continue to extract a democratic peace from the enemy: "The day has come to conquer or submit; if we stand together, victory is certain and the liberty which victory will secure."[50]

In the note to Miliukov, Wilson referred to the central problem of war aims. In 1914, both the Allies and the Central Powers had begun an imperialist and annexationist war. With the American entry into the conflict in 1917, Wilson tried to transform the war into a crusade for democracy. But England, France, and Italy never seriously considered altering their war aims; the only group openly endorsing Wilson's demand were the Russian Bolsheviks. Secretary Lansing informed Wilson on 17 May that American peace proposals might cause domestic political conflicts for the Provisional Government:

It would seem that certain phrases uttered by you are being used by the radical socialists (probably under German influence) to force the Provisional Government to declare a policy which will remove the chief incentive to Russian offensive operations, namely control of the Dardanelles and possession of Constantinople. It is an adroit scheme to advance argument of what is the use of Russia continuing the war and why should she not make a separate peace, if neither in territory nor in indemnity she can be compensated for the enormous expenditure of life and money which a vigorous prosecution of the war will entail.[51]

The German offer of restoring the territorial status quo constituted a more rewarding war aim for Russia than the continuation of the war with an uncertain outcome. Even in the case of a victory, Wilson's calls for a nonannexationist peace would have denied Russia any territorial expansion. A revision of Allied war aims allowing territorial annexations was unacceptable to Wilson. It would have eliminated one of the most important parts of his liberal-democratic peace program. And it would have left the Russian socialists, whom Wilson considered as conspirators with Germany, as the only representatives of nonannexationist war aims. In his note to Miliukov of 22 May, Wilson ignored this dilemma and only referred to war aims in general terms: "No people must be forced under sovereignty under which it does not wish to live. No territory must change hands. . . . No indemnities must be insisted on."[52]

Wilson never persuaded any European government, including the Russian Provisional Government, that the world war had to be continued without expectation of any material or territorial compensations for their efforts and losses. The note of 22 May was an attempt by the president to convince Russian politicians of the American position. Another part of the American policy toward Russia from March through November 1917 involved direct negotiations with the new government with the goal of securing future Russian participation in the war.

In April, Lansing suggested sending a small American delegation to Russia to confer with that country's new leadership. Wilson immediately agreed with the idea and asked him to compile a list of potential participants for the mission. The president insisted that all delegates "should be genuinely enthusiastic for the success of the Russian revolution."[53] Over the course of the following days, Wilson and Lansing exchanged their views on a number of candidates. On Secretary of the Treasury William J. McAdoo's urging, Wilson nominated former Secretary of State and Secretary of War Elihu Root to head the delegation. In selecting the other participants, Wilson tried to include representatives of various political and social groups. As "counterweight" to the conservative Root, Wilson invited James Duncan, vice-president of the American Federation of Labor, and Charles Edward Russell, a liberal-socialist journalist, to join the mission. The delegation was completed by Charles R. Crane, a retired Chicago manufacturer, Cyrus H. McCormick of International Harvester, New York banker Samuel R. Bertron, John R. Mott of the YMCA, Army General Hugh L. Scott, and Admiral James H. Glennon.[54]

Root, who had become a corporate lawyer after ending his political career, was already seventy-two years old when Wilson urged him to undertake the arduous trip halfway around the world from New York via Seattle and Vladivistok to Petrograd. Root was no specialist on Russian affairs, did not speak the language, and made it clear that he only accepted Wilson's invitation reluctantly.

"You have no idea how I hate it," he wrote to former President William Howard Taft on 30 April.[55]

Root was not the only one who had misgivings about his nomination. American liberal and socialist groups resented his selection. Colonel House told the president in early May that the suggestion of Root for the Russian Commission had "raised something of a storm of criticism among the ultra liberals throughout the country." The composition of the delegation suggested to some observers that "it is to be sent to Russia for the commercial benefit of America and not to steady the republic there."[56] Root's biographer Philip C. Jessup admits that it was "not clear" why Wilson selected Root. Jessup suggests that the president believed that Root fulfilled the requirement of being a "real friend of the revolution"— which at that time still meant a revolution that had brought a conservative-democratic government into power. As Jessup further points out, the president was opposed to selecting the other leading candidate for heading the delegation, former president Theodore Roosevelt.[57]

The goal of the Root mission was never exactly specified. The Russian hosts were expected to determine the agenda of the talks with their American visitors. Root's main task was to listen to the Provisional Government's concerns and to assure Russian politicians of the continuing sympathy of the American people for their continued war effort. Root's only clear instruction was that he was not to discuss the important issue of peace terms while he was in Russia.[58]

Shortly before Root arrived in Petrograd, Secretary Lansing cabled the Russian foreign ministry that the American commission was prepared, if the Russian government desired, "to confer upon the best ways and means to bring about effective cooperation between the two Governments in the prosecution of the war against the German autocracy which is to-day the gravest menace to all democratic governments."[59] In other words, Root was expected to talk about ways to help keep Russia in the war but was not allowed to discuss issues pertaining to ending the war.

The Root delegation started its journey on 18 May 1917 and arrived in Petrograd almost four weeks later. During their month-long stay in Russia, the delegates had numerous conversations with members of the Provisional Government in Petrograd and Moscow.

None of the members of the mission, however, met with Lenin or any other leading Bolshevik politicians.[60]

While in Russia, Root sent frequent cables to the State Department, informing Washington about local conditions and about his activities. His estimates of the Provisional Government's chances for survival were at best uncertain, but his expectations about Russian contributions to the war were clearly bleak: "[W]e have found here an infant class in the art of being free containing one hundred and seventy million people and they need to be supplied with kindergarten material; they are sincere, kindly, good people but confused and dazed." In Root's eyes, the fundamental military problem was that the soldiers believed that freedom meant that every man could do as he pleased, including refusing to obey orders. Military discipline "has practically failed," he wrote. The troops did not understand the importance of continuing the war. One factor aggravating the situation was a "tremendous German propaganda" at the front and by "thousands of German agents throughout the country." Those German agents were aided by "extreme socialists who are for peace at any price and very active."[61]

On 17 June, Root requested authorization to release $100,000 for the immediate distribution of pamphlets about Germany's true aims in the war. On 7 July, three weeks after the request and shortly before the mission left Petrograd to return to the United States, the State Department cabled Root that the president had authorized $30,000, less than a third of the requested sum, for propaganda purposes.[62]

In the final report submitted in August 1917, the commission reiterated its warning that internal conflicts might make further Russian contributions to the joint war effort impossible. The commission was satisfied that the Provisional Government wanted to fulfill its war obligations. But it seemed doubtful whether it could maintain power for long, whether the army would continue obeying government orders, and whether a continuous supply of arms and ammunition for the military could be secured. Those problems were increased by the German propaganda in Russia which distributed newspapers and leaflets urging the Russian soldiers to put down their arms. German propagandists, as the commission put it, "spent money like water in the secret purchase of adherents; they bought and established newspapers; . . . they traversed the country and sought to make the simple-minded peasant believe that they only had to stop fighting and take possession of all land in Russia to live in affluence forever after."[63]

Root's report made the basic dilemma of the American policy toward Russia clear. The Wilson administration's goals were, first and foremost, to ensure Russian cooperation in the war and only in the second place to maintain a democratic regime in Petrograd. During his visit to Russia, Root tried to convince the Provisional Government that there was no contradiction between those two goals. An objective of the Root mission was to "promote a realization of the fact that the effective continuance of the war was the only course by which the opportunity for Russia to work out the conditions of her own freedom could be preserved from destruction by German domination."[64] The ministers of the Provisional Government agreed with him in public statements. A growing majority of Russian front soldiers and a group of revolutionaries in Petrograd, however, considered a continued war effort to be only in the interest of the Western Allies.

The Root commission submitted two specific proposals aimed at increasing the long-term fighting abilities of the Russian army. First, extended American propaganda efforts should counterbalance the German influence. A news agency should spread information about the United States in Russia. Second, the fighting morale of the soldiers should be increased by establishing a Russian YMCA.[65] None of these plans could be put into effect, however, before the October Revolution.

Wilson, too, saw the need to counterbalance German propaganda and on 23 October sent Edgar G. Sisson, a former city editor of the *Chicago Tribune* who had joined George Creel's Committee on Public Information, to Petrograd to open an information and propaganda agency. But this move came too late. Even before Sisson arrived in Russia, the Bolshevik coup d'état of November 1917 had toppled the Provisional Government.[66]

The commission's suggestions were hardly suitable for neutralizing the revolutionary potential in Russia. It appears that Root himself was aware of the shortcomings of his suggestions. While in Russia, he urged the Provisional Government repeatedly to take stronger measures against the domestic opposition: "I [Root] had information (while in Petrograd) about what Lenin was doing and I urged the Provisional Government to arrest him."[67] After Russian newspapers had printed reports about forthcoming police actions against the Bolsheviks, Lenin fled from Petrograd and only returned shortly before the October Revolution.

While it was not clear in April why Wilson chose to dispatch Root to Russia, the president's behavior during Root's journey and after his envoy's return was even more difficult to understand. The president presumably would send an emissary whose judgment he trusted and whom he would consult for future decisions. Wilson did neither. He ignored Root's request for immediate release of funds while he was in Russia and met with him only once after his return. The president was under the false impression that he himself knew how to handle threats to democracy in foreign states. He was not looking for advice when he sent Root to Russia, but for reconfirmation of his own views that Russian democracy, though challenged by a small group of revolutionaries, would undoubtedly survive.[68]

The dispatch of the Root commission and of Edgar Sisson to Russia constituted important parts of the United States' support for the Provisional Government. American experts were sent to help Russia continue its war efforts. Washington also provided financial assistance. In mid-May 1917, the Department of the Treasury granted the Provisional Government a first loan of $100 million. The condition of the loan was continued Russian participation in the war: "In case of discontinuance of war the credit will of course cease to be extended." In meetings with members of the Provisional Government, Ambassador Francis repeatedly emphasized the linkage between U.S. support and the continuance of the war. In mid-April, he told Finance Minister Mikhail I. Tereshchenko that "no aid whatever would be extended if separate peace concluded." On the eve of the October Revolution, the United States had granted Russia credits amounting to $325 million, of which Russia had already spent almost $200 million.[69]

In granting credits, the United States possessed a powerful tool to influence Russian policy and improve Russia's capacity to continue fighting. In July 1917, for example, Russian soldiers in Finland refused to accept Russian rubles as payment and threatened mutiny. An American credit of $75 million brought them back into the war.[70]

The United States granted the financial support out of a realization of the importance of Russia's continued participation in the war. A termination of Allied support would most likely have led to an immediate collapse of the Eastern front. The military effects of such a collapse would have been far reaching. Germany would be able to relocate up to eighty divisions from the East to the Western front where inexperienced American troops were about to enter the conflict. In exchange for their financial commitment to Russia, the Allies insisted that the Provisional Government would not agree to separate peace negotiations with Germany but would continue fighting the war.

From a military point of view, Russia should have capitulated in the summer of 1917. The army was spiritually and materially incapable of continuing the war. In a memorandum of 18 (31) March 1917, General Aleksandr S. Lukomskii, director of military operations, informed the government about the conditions of the army:

The army is undergoing [a period of] sickness. It will take probably two or three months to readjust the relations between officers and men. At the present time one observes low spirits among the officer personnel, unrest among the troops, and a great number of desertions. . . . It is now impossible to carry out the offensive operations which had been planned for in the spring. . . . The Government should quite definitely and clearly advise our allies of all this, pointing out that now we are not in a position to carry out the engagement entered into at the conferences of Chantilly and Petrograd.[71]

But France and Great Britain were not prepared to free Russia from its obligations as an ally. General Robert George Nivelle, commander-in-chief of the French army, insisted on Russian participation in the planned spring offensive: "I request the Russian army to render the greatest possible assistance in the operations which have already been begun by the Anglo-French armies."[72]

In June the Provisional Government agreed to take part in the planned Allied offensive. On 16 (29) June, Alexander Kerensky, the newly appointed defense minister, signed the order. The Russian participation was explained as a measure supporting the Allies in their war efforts on the Western front. Colonel Jakubovic, assistant secretary of war, declared on 14 (27) May that Germany was currently transferring troops from the Eastern to the Western front because Berlin did not anticipate a Russian attack:

At the present moment all is perfectly quiet on the Russian front. Taking advantage of this, our enemy now transfers his forces to the front of our

French and English allies. He is even transferring heavy artillery over there, replacing it on our front by our own artillery pieces, of old make, taken at Osovets and Kovno.[73]

The Russian offensive of 1917, therefore, was not a reaction to an immediate threat from Germany. The attack on the Eastern front was meant to involve Germany in new battles on Russian soil. It was questionable whether such a policy was in Russia's and in the Allies' best interest. It could lead to a complete collapse of the army and to Russia's permanent withdrawal from fighting. The military leadership of the country repeatedly warned about the effects of the attack.

Why would the Provisional Government take part in a new military offensive? Alexander Kerensky, in charge of the decision to start the offensive, wrote in the introduction to a 1961 document collection about the history of the Provisional Government that the new campaign was directed mainly at uniting all Russian factions in the battle against the common foreign enemy. The beginning of the war in 1914, Kerensky wrote, "had signaled a great upsurge of national feeling and loyalty to the throne. Turning from its preoccupation with mounting internal grievances and disagreements, the nation united in the struggle against the foreign enemy." In the summer of 1917, Kerensky tried to reunite the people in the fight for democracy. He attempted to counterbalance the Bolshevik antiwar propaganda with a positive war aim, the victory over Germany. The continuation of the war was aimed at diverting the soldiers' and the public's attention from the internal problems of the country. In the words of historian Arno Mayer, while Lenin wanted to continue the revolution to end the war, Kerensky was forced "to continue the war in order to crush the (Bolshevik) Revolution."[74]

The Russian offensive started on 18 (31) June. During the first few days, the army was surprisingly successful and achieved considerable territorial gains in eastern Galicia. In mid-July, however, the Russian advance came to a halt. After the beginning of the German counteroffensive on 19 July, Russian troops lost most of their territorial gains within a few days. The military defeat had a destabilizing effect on the political situation in Russia. The German advance, as the leadership of the Russian 11th Army stated in a cable from 9 (22) July 1917, was "assuming the character of a disaster which threatens a catastrophe to revolutionary Russia. . . . Most of the military units are in a state of complete disorganization, . . . and they no longer listen to the orders of their leaders."[75]

Kerensky's attempt to neutralize the Bolshevik antiwar propaganda with a successful military campaign had failed. Prime Minister L'vov resigned in its wake. In the streets of Petrograd demonstrators demanded "All Power to the Soviets." Kerensky, who succeeded L'vov as prime minister, faced a steadily growing war-weariness among the population. Russia's primarily rural population and its proletariat were interested neither in an expansionist war nor in a crusade for democracy. The masses were only concerned about a quick ending of the war and an implementation of the promised land reform. The only party in Petrograd to advocate those popular goals were the Bolsheviks.

Most Western historians today agree that the Allies' refusal to relieve Russia from its military obligation in the summer of 1917 contributed to the overthrow of the Provisional Government. George F. Kennan wrote that the reason for the breakdown of the Russian political structure in early 1917 and for the ensuing degeneration during the following months into the "rigidities and extremism of Bolshevism" was the world war. Whatever the Western Allies were fighting for, they sacrificed Russia's real needs in these crucial years for those aims. "The Russian Revolution and the alienation of the Russian people from the Western community for decades to come were only a part of the staggering price paid by the Western people for their insistence on completing a military victory over Germany in 1917 and 1918."[76]

The question that arises is whether Wilson and Lansing made a conscious decision in the summer of 1917 to give greater priority to a continuing Russian military engagement than to a potential democratic development of the country. Did they sacrifice Russian democracy for the sake of short-term military assistance? It appears that the question has to be answered in the negative for both the president and the secretary of state, though for different reasons. In the summer of 1917, Lansing was skeptical about both the Russian democracy's chances of survival and the possibility of its future participation in the war. After a conversation with Elihu Root in August, he wrote that Prime Minister Kerensky had granted the Bolsheviks far too many concessions. The United States had to prepare for the time "when Russia will no longer be a factor in the war."[77] Lansing, in other words, expected the Provisional Government to collapse regardless of continued Russian participation in the war.

Wilson, on the other hand, does not appear to have expected an overthrow of the Provisional Government in 1917. In March, he expressed his fear that the Russian people might try to end the war as soon as possible after they had forced the tsar's abdication. In late summer, that fear had given way to the view that continuing participation in the war was a *sine qua non* for Russian democracy. He hoped to convince the Russians that the overthrow of the tsar was merely the first step toward establishing a true democracy. On 23 October, two weeks before the Bolshevik coup d'état, he assured the "newborn" Russian democracy of the friendship of the older American democracy: "The war aspects [will] take care of themselves if a band . . . [is] forged between the Russian and the American people."[78] On the same day that the Bolsheviks took over power in Russia, Charles Edward Russell, a member of the Root mission, confirmed Wilson in that attitude: "The typical Russian acknowledges no obligation on the part of Russia to the Allies; he only acknowledges the duty of a democrat to fight for democracy." Russell suggested intensifying the American propaganda efforts in Russia, especially about the democratic war aims. "If it is addressed to the Russian's passion for democracy, and if it shows him that his beloved Revolution is in peril, he will be ready to fight with all his strength, and there is no better fighter in the world." Wilson agreed with that interpretation about the Russian conditions. In his reply to Russell, he wrote that the analysis presented to him "runs along the lines of my own thought, only you speak from knowledge and I have thought by inference, and you may be sure that I will do my best to act along the lines it suggests, though all sorts of work in Russia now is rendered extremely difficult because no one channel connects with the other, apparently."[79]

The idea of a revolution in a democratic country aimed at overthrowing elected leaders was contrary to Wilson's historical and philosophical views about the general political development toward democracy. If democracy was threatened in Russia, it was not threatened by the people, but by a small clique of traitors acting in its own interest. But since the Russian people had succeeded in overthrowing an undemocratic rule before, Wilson was optimistic that the country would return to democracy after the Bolshevik coup d'état: "I have not lost faith in the Russian outcome by any means." Wilson wrote to Congressman Frank Clark one week after the October Revolution, "Russia, like France in the past century, will no doubt have to go through deep waters but she will come out upon firm land on the other side and her great people, for they are a great people, will in my opinion take their proper place in the world."[80]

The letter to Clark expressed the ideological principles that would serve as the basis for Wilson's Soviet policy after November 1917: the rejection of the Bolshevik government, and his conviction that the socialist rule would only be temporary because it did not reflect the true will of the Russian people and would be overthrown without outside assistance. Similar to the decision to enter into World War I, Wilson's initial ideological conviction was soon challenged by the political demands by the governments in London and Paris. The Allies rejected the American positions on both the war and Soviet policy questions and pushed Wilson into accepting a less ideological and more pragmatic policy.

2

"Without Annexations and Contributions": Wilson, Lenin, and the War-Aims Question

[T]he whole state of sentiment in Russia is so confused and even problematical that I have found nothing more difficult than determining what course would be best to pursue.
— Woodrow Wilson to Edward Woods, 17 April 1918.[1]

The years of Woodrow Wilson's presidency were a tumultuous era in international relations. Revolutions and wars in Central America, Asia, and Europe forced the president to devote considerable time and energy in response to foreign political problems. The issues he faced in those conflicts, moreover, concerned very fundamental political and social issues, such as overcoming the heritage of imperialist domination of China and reacting to socially and economically motivated uprisings in Mexico and Russia. Contemporary comments by Wilson show that he was well aware of the importance of the uprisings at the time. In an August 1914 letter to Secretary of War Lindley M. Garrison, for example, he compared the Mexican rebellion to the French Revolution. In his letter to Congressman Frank Clark of November 1917, he emphasized the parallels between the French and the Russian October revolutions.[2]

Wilson's comparison of events in Mexico and Russia to the French Revolution yields some insights into the president's thinking about the uprisings he witnessed. The revolution of 1789 and the earlier American Revolution stood out in modern political history as cataclysmic events that shook off old systems of colonialism and monarchy in favor of more enlightened principles, such as republicanism and guaranteeing the rights of the citizens. But instead of emphasizing the similarities between the American and the French revolutions in his writings, Wilson pointed to what he considered the fundamental differences between those two historic revolutions. His views about the French Revolution stood in the tradition of Edmund Burke whose *Reflections on the Revolution in France* claimed that the revolution went wrong when it attempted to create a completely new political system overnight. Instead of creating a new order, the dissolution of the feudal institutions led to confusion and to the Terror. Wilson distinguished between the French Revolution, whose principles he rejected, and the American, which he welcomed: "There is almost nothing in common between popular outbreaks such as took place in France at her great Revolution and the establishment of a government like our own." Democracy in Europe, he continued, "has acted always in rebellion, as a destructive force." In contrast, in America, democracy had an "organic growth." There was "nothing revolutionary in its movements; it had not to overthrow other polities; it had only to organize itself. It had not to create, but only to expand, self-government."[3]

Comparing current episodes of unrest to the French Revolution, therefore, not only indicated Wilson's belief in the historical significance of those events, but also showed his disdain for those actions. He considered the October Revolution in Russia a prime example of a reprehensible uprising. The goal of the revolution was to overthrow a democratic government, replacing it with a dictatorship of the proletariat and eventually destroying all nation-states in favor of creating a single-state and classless society. In Wilson's diametrically opposed view, democratic governments should stand at the helm of nation-states. Wilson rejected the Bolshevik uprising as a coup d'état not only because of the small number of active revolutionaries, but also because of the goals to which they aspired. His own political aims were evolutionary rather than revolutionary. Governments, he maintained, "have never been successfully and permanently changed except by slow modification operating from generation to generation."[4] The old European political struggles should give way to more democratic forms of international affairs.

A crucial aspect for the understanding of Wilson's Soviet policy was the rejection of the Bolshevik regime immediately after the October Revolution. His refusal to enter into official relations with Lenin was not the result of specific actions of the Soviets while they were in power, such as the dismissal of the Constituent Assembly in January 1918, but was based on ideological reasons. In his policy-centered view, Wilson neglected economic considerations that played an important part in the decisions of the Russian masses to join radical socialist groups in 1917. Russian peasants turned away from the Provisional Government because L'vov continued the war and rejected the implementation of a land reform. The masses supported the Bolsheviks who promised to end the war and to redistribute the land.

Did Wilson's rejection of Bolshevik ideology necessitate an active intervention in Russian affairs? Wilson's philosophical and political thinking suggests "no." In his August 1914 letter to Garrison about the events in Mexico, he wrote that it would not be right for the United States to direct by force the "internal processes of what is a profound revolution, a revolution as profound as that which occurred in France." In his letter to Clark he expressed his anticipation that Russia would soon turn toward democracy again.

To understand Wilson's Russian policy after the October Revolution, it is insufficient to look only at the ideological confrontation with the Bolsheviks; one also has to examine decisions concerning Russia in the context of America's political alliances. Ideological arguments compelled the president to sever relations with the Bolsheviks, but not to intervene in Russian affairs, while the governments in London and Paris urged Wilson to adopt an actively anti-Soviet policy.

By the time of the October Revolution in 1917, the world war still commanded most of the attention of U.S. and European politicians and military planners. In April 1917, President Wilson had committed the United States to achieving victory in the conflict. But with less than 100,000 men in Europe in the fall of 1917, the American Expeditionary Force (AEF) was still far from reaching strength sufficient to turn the tide of the war. It was only in the spring and summer of 1918 that between 250,000 and 300,000 men landed in France each month, eventually totaling 2 million.[5] During that period of increasing U.S. involvement in

Europe, the October Revolution occurred in Russia, after which a new revolutionary regime led by Lenin proposed an immediate cease-fire and peace negotiations to both warring alliances. The Western refusal to accept an immediate peace led to ideological, propaganda, and military conflicts between the Western powers and Soviet Russia. Once the Western Allies had started to look upon Russia's new rulers as traitors and agents of Imperial Germany, they failed to perceive changes in the Soviet foreign policy beginning in February and March of 1918.

As Russia's enemy in the world war, the Imperial German government followed the events in Petrograd in 1917 with greatest interest. Berlin saw the political unrest there in terms of a military weakening of its enemy. The political conflicts were bound to affect the Russian army at a time when the overall military situation for the Central Powers was far from satisfactory. Germany's initial military strategy under the Schlieffen Plan in the summer of 1914 had called for a quick victory against France in the West that would allow the *Reichswehr* to deploy the full strength of its forces against Russia in the East. The goal was to avoid a protracted two-front war. Following the attack in the West, however, the front there had turned into a system of trenches without any prospect of immediate victory and forced the German high military command to conduct the two-front war it had hoped to avoid. By the spring of 1917, the United States had entered the war on the side of the Allies and was steadily increasing its troop contingents in Europe. If Germany could negotiate a favorable separate peace agreement with a weakened Russia, it would achieve its war aims in the East and would be free to send its Russian armies to support the war in France.

Since the beginning of the war in 1914, the German foreign ministry had developed plans aimed at breaking up the Entente to free Germany from the encirclement. Under Secretary of State Arthur Zimmermann wrote in a memorandum in late November 1914 that to achieve an "honorable" and "lasting" peace it might be "desirable that a wedge should be driven between our enemies, so that we may conclude an early separate peace with one or the other." Initially, those plans to undermine the Entente were not only directed against Russia, but also against France. Moreover, the policy toward Russia was aimed both at improving relations with the Imperial government, with the goal of concluding a separate peace treaty, and at encouraging domestic opposition, particularly anti-Russian nationalistic groups. The most successful effort in undermining the Russian war effort, however, was in supporting the socialist opposition in Russia and in exile.[6]

In the spring of 1917, the February Revolution put Russia's future military effectiveness into question. After Russian Foreign Minister Pavel Miliukov's statement of March 1917 that the Provisional Government would continue its war efforts, German diplomats suggested supporting the radical revolutionary parties in Russia. At the same time, the German government received reports that Lenin and other Russian socialists living in exile in Switzerland were requesting passage through Germany to Russia.

Lenin's name appeared in German documents pertaining to separate peace negotiations early in the war. In September 1915, the German minister in Bern, Count Romberg, had reported about a seven-point peace program Lenin advocated that included an immediate Russian offer of peace on the basis of no annexations and no demands of war reparations. In early 1917, the military high command and the foreign ministry were in agreement that Lenin's return to Russia should be facilitated to undermine the country's war efforts and to bring about peace on the Eastern front. In mid-April, Lenin and thirty fellow comrades traveled from Zurich to Stockholm in a "sealed" train car. From Stockholm he journeyed to Petrograd where he arrived on 3 (16) April.[7]

By the time of the outbreak of the First World War, Lenin had been the foremost theoretician of the radical Russian Bolshevik party for over a decade. He had applied traditional Marxist philosophy to the political and economic conditions in Russia and had redefined the role of the intellectual avant-garde in a socialist revolution. Both interpretations were crucial for undertaking a socialist revolution in Russia. Lenin disagreed with the prevailing view among Marxists at the time that the agrarian and feudal Russian economy of the late nineteenth century would first have to undergo a capitalist transformation before a socialist revolution could be successful. From a statistical analysis of living conditions in rural Russia at the turn of the century, Lenin concluded that there already existed the class distinction into a bourgeoisie (landowning peasants) and a proletariat (landless peasants) that characterized capitalist societies and that was believed to be necessary for a successful socialist revolution. In a pamphlet entitled *What Is to Be Done?*, published in March 1902, Lenin also broke with the traditional Marxist view about the road leading to a socialist revolution. Marxist tradition had put the workers in the center of the revolutionary movement and had granted socialist political parties only an indirect role in the revolutionary process as tutors to help the proletariat develop its class consciousness. Lenin reversed those roles. He saw the intellectual in the center of the revolution as the leader of the proletariat in its revolutionary struggles.

Lenin's *Letters from Afar*, written between the February Revolution of 1917 and his return to Petrograd in April of that year, reveal his urgent desire to influence events in Russia out of fear that a leaderless proletariat might miss a revolutionary opportunity. From the start, Lenin looked upon the February Revolution as merely a precursor for a second, socialist, uprising. That socialist revolution had become inevitable with the outbreak of the First World War, the "imperialist war," in Lenin's dictum. He interpreted the world war as a conflict between two hostile imperialist camps for global economic and military predominance that was fought on the backs of the working classes. The war, he believed, would inevitably create a revolutionary situation that would lead to the end of capitalism. The bourgeoisie would be unable to "delay for long the revolutionary crisis" that was "growing with irresistible force in all countries, beginning with Germany . . . and ending with England and France." Lenin saw his task in this revolutionary process as transforming the war into a civil war in the imperialist states. In March 1917, he outlined the revolutionary process after a socialist revolution had brought political power into the hands of the Soviets. An All-Russia Soviet would declare that it was not bound by any treaty concluded by the bourgeois governments. Then it would publish all secret treaties concerning their expansionist war aims, would urge all belligerents to conclude an immediate armistice, and would call upon the workers of all countries to overthrow their bourgeois governments.[8]

In his *Letters from Afar*, Lenin not only called for revolutions abroad, but also pledged Russian support for revolutionary wars. The Soviets would "wage war against any bourgeois government and against all bourgeois governments of the world, because this would really be a just war, because all the workers and toilers in all countries would ask for its success." In his analysis of Lenin's calls for revolutionary war up to April 1917, however, historian

Robert Service found those calls so unspecific that they have to be considered "slogans" rather than a "fully elaborated policy." After his return to Petrograd, moreover, until the October Revolution, Lenin rarely wrote or talked about "revolutionary war." And in early 1918, during the Brest-Litovsk peace talks with Imperial Germany, he made it clear that he did not expect a revolutionary war against Germany to be successful.[9] Instead, Lenin's revolutionary internationalism was of only secondary importance to his revolutionary domestic political program. All goals the Bolsheviks might harbor depended on launching a successful revolution in Russia and on maintaining power afterward.

In his calls for an immediate end to the war, Lenin represented exactly the kind of revolutionary who, as the German government hoped, could destroy Russia's determination to continue the war. German Foreign Minister Richard von Kühlmann noted shortly after the October Revolution that the "disruption of the Entente and the subsequent creation of political combinations agreeable to us constitute the most important war aim of our diplomacy." Russia, Kühlmann believed, had been the weakest partner of the Entente. And he revealed to what extent he believed German support was necessary for the success of the October Revolution: "It was not until the Bolsheviks had received from us a steady flow of funds through various channels and under varying labels that they were in a position to be able to build up their main organ, *Pravda*, to conduct energetic propaganda and appreciably to extend the originally narrow basis of their party."[10]

Lenin, nevertheless, was no German "agent," that is, representing solely German interests. On the contrary, he pursued his own agenda which focused on socialist revolutions in Russia and in Germany and on peace on his own terms. Some contemporaries in the Allied states argued during and after the war that the true goal of the Bolsheviks was the conclusion of a separate German-Soviet peace treaty. The Soviets, however, never called for a separate peace treaty and would have preferred a general and immediate cessation of all hostilities. That charge of advocating a separate peace also disregards the Soviet negotiating behavior at the Brest-Litovsk peace talks and the internal Bolshevik controversy that erupted in the winter of 1917/18 about whether or not to accept the harsh German conditions for peace. Lenin was opportunistic enough to accept support from his political opponent, Imperial Germany, to reach his goals.[11]

Immediately after his arrival in Petrograd, Lenin announced a radical political program, the so-called April Theses, in which he urged the workers not to support the Provisional Government and its war efforts any longer: "In our attitude toward the war not the slightest concession must be made to 'revolutionary defencism' [i.e., the revolutionary proletariat defending the bourgeois state], for under the new government of L'vov and Co., owing to the capitalist nature of this government, the war on Russia's part remains a predatory imperialist war." The present situation, Lenin went on, represented a "transition" from the first stage of the revolution, leading to the assumption of power by the "bourgeoisie," to the second stage "which is to place power in the hands of the proletariat."[12]

Lenin's position on the question of war and peace differed from Wilson's in one important respect. Like Lenin, Wilson, too, had initially criticized the war. He had then found reason to support one side in the conflict over the other to achieve his ultimate goal of a democratic peace. During the months of American participation in the war, however, Wilson was compelled to compromise with his conservative Allies, Great Britain and France, in the war-aims question. But Lenin continued to view the war in ideological terms and made his radical and uncompromising position clear from the outset. He interpreted the aims of the warring countries in terms of internal class antagonism. To satisfy the interests of the capitalists, they would send peasants and workers to the battlefields. Wilson believed that industrialists and workers in the United States had a common interest in achieving victory in the war. In his war message speech of 2 April, he had urged the laborers to defend America's freedom. Wilson believed he was waging a just war; to Lenin the only just war was the workers' battle for the introduction of socialism.

After his return to Petrograd, Lenin was initially an extremist on the left fringes of the Russian political spectrum. His views concerning both Russia's readiness for a socialist revolution and the role of the party were hotly disputed among Russian socialists before the October Revolution. In the spring and summer of 1917, only the most radical parties followed his views on war and peace and on imminent socialist revolutions. The American consul in

Petrograd, Winship, described Lenin's isolated position in a cable to the State Department on 30 April. He reported that the Council of Workmen's and Soldiers' Deputies had called Lenin's propaganda "dangerous and counterrevolutionary." That resolution, Winship added, would force Lenin to openly oppose the Council and deprive him and his followers of authority among many workers and soldiers.[13]

The Bolshevik success in November 1917 was as much the result of Lenin's persistence as it was testimony to the Provisional Government's inability to react to the radicalization of the public mood in Russia. L'vov's rejection of an immediate land reform and his refusal to end the war increased the popularity of the radical socialist parties, including the Bolsheviks, over the summer. The Provisional Government was viewed as serving foreign as opposed to Russian interests. Winship noted in May 1917: "The socialistic masses feel that Milyukov, and more indirectly the Temporary Government, is acceptable to the Allies and is willing, if not anxious, to force Russia to fight the Allies' battle."[14]

In the elections in the fall of 1917, the Bolsheviks for the first time won a majority of delegates in the Petrograd Soviet. That was the sign for Lenin to start the revolt against the Provisional Government. On 13 (26) September, he wrote that "the Bolsheviks, having obtained a majority in the Soviets of Workers' and Soldiers' Deputies of both capitals, can and *must* take state power into their own hands." Lenin knew that the Provisional Government's reluctance to redistribute land and to end the war had led to the radicalization of the workers. He was eager to prevent the loss of popular support and implemented his program immediately.[15] The centerpiece of the Bolshevik coup d'état of 25 October (7 November) 1917 was the arrest of the Provisional Government in the Winter Palace. In the early morning hours of 26 October (8 November) the Bolsheviks, who had laid siege to the Palace for hours, gained entry and arrested the ministers.[16]

Even before the revolution, Lenin was convinced that the future success for his policy relied on the speedy implementation of his political and economic promises. This conviction was responsible for the Bolsheviks' immediate decision after the revolution to start peace negotiations. Lenin had to end the war for political, economic, and ideological reasons. Lenin's policy immediately after the revolution was designed to consolidate power in the hands of the Bolsheviks. On the day of the revolution, the Bolshevik majority of the Second All-Russian Congress of Soviets elected Lenin president and Leon Trotsky commissar for foreign affairs. It also passed decrees that sanctioned the coup d'état and marked the beginning of a new Russian policy.[17] In the *Decree on Peace*, the Congress of Soviets urged all war-waging parties to abandon their annexationist war aims and to start immediate negotiations for a just and democratic peace. The *Decree on Land* ordered the expropriation of all great landowners without compensation.

Western historiography is split over whether the development from a democratic to a socialist Russian republic was an accidental development or whether it was already implicit in the February Revolution. Conservative historians consider the October Revolution an aberration from the path to liberty that was begun in February. Historian Karl-Heinz Ruffmann, for example, believes that the turn toward socialism was anything but inevitable. The prime forces in that process were "Lenin's desire to rule and the mistakes and weaknesses of his opponents . . . in a crisis situation that had grown during the war." Liberal historians consider the events of February and October merely as steps constituting one revolution which, like most revolutions after 1789, underwent a period of radicalization after the period of initial success. Historian Dietrich Geyer doubts that the Russian bourgeoisie of 1917 could have created a truly democratic government:

The narrow social strata whose political convictions most closely approximated "democracy" as understood in the West had hoped for as quiet and painless a cabinet reshuffle as possible in order to effect the transfer of power to the Duma. After the collapse of the monarchy, however, large sections of the population began to intervene in political affairs. . . . The politically informed sector of tsarist society was forced to embrace democratic policies whose underlying concepts and standards were not its own. . . . The Revolution . . . possessed an inner dynamic which could not be controlled. This dilemma was in evidence from the outset in the confrontation between the soviets and the Provisional Government.[18]

On the eve of the October Revolution, Russia was divided into two opposing social camps—the nobility and industrialists on the one hand, and peasants and workers on the other. Neither group harbored democratic ideals. The goal of the Wilson administration after November 1917 to help the Russians create a truly democratic government indicated the president's high goals, but appears unrealistic and self-defeating with regard to the Russian situation.

The Allied-Russian conflict about ending the war started in the wake of the publication of the *Decree on Peace*. In that decree, the Congress of Soviets urged immediate peace negotiations and rejected all annexationist war aims:

An overwhelming majority of the workers and the labouring classes of all the belligerent countries, exhausted, tormented, and racked by war, are longing for a just and democratic peace—a peace which in the most definite and insistent manner has been demanded by the Russian workers and peasants since the overthrow of the Tsarist monarchy. By such a peace the Government understands an immediate peace without annexations . . . and without indemnities.[19]

The Bolsheviks challenged Wilson by issuing peace initiatives in which they called for a democratic peace while at the same time alleging that the United States entered the war for economic and imperialist reasons. On 8 (21) November, Trotsky declared at a meeting of the Central Executive Committee of the Bolshevik party that the United States entered the war "under the influence of the sober calculations of the American Stock Exchange." He claimed that the United States had joined the Entente because its exports, which had doubled during the war, were threatened by the German U-boats. Trotsky declared that the administration was interested primarily in a weakening of both coalitions to consolidate, what he called, the "hegemony of American capital."[20] After the American entry into the war, a recent presidential biographer noted, Wilson "could no longer approve what he himself had said earlier" about a peace without victory. In the fall of 1917, that formula was revived by the Russian socialists.[21]

On the same day that Trotsky charged that the United States entered the war for economic interests, he also submitted an official invitation to the ambassadors of the Western Allies in Petrograd to begin immediate armistice negotiations.[22]

The Soviets followed a double strategy in the peace question that at first glance appears contradictory. In the *Decree on Peace* they urged the Entente and Central Powers to open negotiations with them, but at the same time appealed to the proletariat of those states to overthrow their governments. The Soviets offered immediate armistice negotiations out of the realization that Russia was exhausted from the war and was unable to resist German attacks any longer. But at the same time, the Soviets made it as embarrassing as possible for the Western Allies to accept the proposed terms. Historians have come to see the attempt to discredit the Allies' "imperialist" war aims as the overriding aspect of the *Decree on Peace*. George F. Kennan called the *Decree* the first example of "demonstrative diplomacy," that is, diplomacy designed to "embarrass other governments and stir up opposition among their own people."[23]

There appears to be only one explanation for the Soviet strategy in the peace question: The Bolsheviks believed that neither the Entente nor the Central Powers would sign an immediate peace treaty. Lenin, however, did not want to conclude a costly and humiliating separate treaty with Imperial Germany, and hoped that the workers in Germany and England would soon follow the Russian example and take over power in their countries. Only after socialist revolutions in Western Europe had established "anti-imperialist" governments would it be possible to conclude a general nonannexationist peace. Ambassador Francis noted on 28 November that Trotsky "threatens appeals to peoples of countries whose Governments will not recognize him or refuse to propose armistice and peace." On 19 December 1917, four days after the signing of the Russo-German armistice at Brest-Litovsk, Trotsky made it clear that encouraging social revolutions in other countries was the main Soviet goal. He issued an appeal to the "toiling, oppressed, and exhausted peoples of Europe" in which he declared that he did not consider the "existing capitalist Governments capable of making a democratic peace." The Soviet government, therefore, faced a double task. It had to end the war as quickly as possible, and it had "to use all the means at our disposal to help the working class in all lands to overthrow the rule of capital and seize the political power in order to reconstruct Europe and the whole world on democratic and socialist lines." Trotsky then pleaded with the socialists in all countries, "but especially to socialists in Germany," to recognize that the Russian war aims differed from those of the "German capitalists, landowners, and generals."[24]

The Soviet peace strategy in 1917 was a gamble that did not pay off. Revolutions did not occur in Western Europe, and the Soviets faced decidedly anti-Bolshevik negotiators of the Imperial German and Austrian governments at Brest-Litovsk. Trotsky's fiery revolutionary speeches, moreover, made a lasting impression on Western politicians. For generations they considered Soviet foreign policy as bent on encouraging foreign revolutions, despite a reorientation only a few months after the Russian Revolution. When it became clear in late February 1918 that Trotsky's foreign policy approach was unsuccessful, the Soviets changed their approach to the Western Allies.

First reports about the Bolshevik coup d'état reached the United States on 8 November 1917. The following day, U.S. newspapers covered the Russian events in great detail. In an article under the headline, "Kerensky, Deposed, a Fugitive; Radicals Seize Petrograd," the *Washington Post* reported the arrest of members of the Provisional Government. In another article, "Hope in Russians Lost by Diplomats. Frankly Admitted Here More War Help Is Unlikely," the paper addressed the crucial issue of Russia's continued participation in the war: "The fall of Kerensky and the assumption of power by the maximalists who favor an immediate peace has now brought the Russian situation to its maximum danger point. It represents the end of the pendulum's swing towards anarchistic radicalism and pro-German intrigue, according to officials of the United States Government."[25]

By mid-December, the State Department realized the dominant position the Bolsheviks had achieved in Russia. Ambassador David R. Francis cabled to the State Department on 7 December, "think impossible for Soviet government to [last] long." Two weeks later he reversed his opinion: "Bolsheviki have maintained themselves in power in Petrograd and Nankeen (Moscow?) and are *de facto* government in those cities and although there are opposition movements in Ukraine and elsewhere, Bolshevik power is undoubtedly greatest in Russia."[26] Despite that status as de facto government, none of the Allies was prepared to grant the Soviet government diplomatic recognition.

Wilson's policy of supporting the Provisional Government in order to secure Russia's continued participation in the war had failed. A party had seized power in Petrograd that tried to leave the war as soon as possible, and Washington suddenly faced a radically changed situation. The administration's problems were aggravated by the insufficient means of communication with the Russian capital, which made it difficult to obtain precise information about the events there. Reports about the reaction of the Russian military to the coup d'état were especially contradictory. On 12 November, the *Washington Post* reported that "Bolshevik Mob Flees as Kerensky's Troops Enter Tsarskoe Selo." Prime Minister Kerensky, who had left the Winter Palace before the Bolshevik attack, sought support for the Provisional Government among troops from the front. American papers estimated the number of troops loyal to Kerensky to be as high as 200,000. That figure, however, was much too high. Modern estimates put Kerensky's support at less than 20,000 men.[27] On 14 November, American papers announced the victory of Bolshevik troops over Kerensky in the battle of Tsarskoe Selo.

In the winter of 1917/18, Wilson faced the immediate question of whether to oppose the Bolsheviks or to extend diplomatic recognition to their leadership once they had established themselves in power. There were advocates for both positions in the United States. According to the adherents of a confrontational nonrecognition policy, among them Secretary of State Robert Lansing and a majority of State Department officials, the Russian revolutionaries of November 1917 were "agents" of Imperial Germany. As proof, they cited the German permission for Lenin to travel through Germany and the separate peace negotiations going on at Brest-Litovsk. Adherents to the agent theory believed that there should be no cooperation between the United States and the Bolsheviks. Instead, the Wilson administration should consider fighting the Soviet leadership as part of its war effort against Germany. The Allies should support anti-Bolshevik resistance groups, encourage those groups to establish an anti-Soviet government, and, if necessary, intervene in the Russian civil war. After the end of the First World War, that group continued advocating a tough policy toward the Bolsheviks, excluding them, for example, from the proceedings of the Paris Peace Conference and rejecting the idea of recognizing them as the legitimate Russian government.

According to a competing theory, Bolshevism was primarily a social phenomenon. Russian workers and peasants rose against their government because of deteriorating living conditions, not because of a conspiracy with Germany. Adherents to that theory made the United States and the Allies to a certain degree responsible for the October Revolution. Allied and American military planners had insisted on a Russian military offensive in the summer of 1917 despite the Russian army's obvious inability at that late point in the war to pursue such a campaign with any chance of success. The resulting defeat of the Russian troops had a severely demoralizing effect on soldiers and on the population at large and increased the influence of social revolutionary and antiwar activists among the troops. According to the second view, an Allied confrontational policy toward the socialist government in Petrograd would lead to a further increase in popular support for the Bolsheviks. In contrast, a truly anti-Bolshevik policy would be to assure the Russian people of continued Western support, opening political relations with the de facto government and granting Russia economic aid. That idea of cooperation was favored by a small number of State Department officials stationed in Petrograd. In the public debate about future Russian policy, journalists Walter Lippmann and Lincoln Steffens, and William C. Bullitt, a junior State Department official, advocated improved relations with the Soviets.[28]

By late November, Wilson had not made a final decision about how to deal with the Bolsheviks. On the one hand, he was convinced that the Soviet rulers were determined to conclude a separate peace treaty with Germany. The United States had to try to prevent or delay the conclusion of such a treaty. On the other hand, Wilson refused to enter into direct negotiations with the Bolsheviks because that would have implied diplomatic recognition of their regime. The American cabinet discussed the Russian developments in its meeting on 27 November. The minutes of the meeting clearly demonstrate Wilson's desire to prevent having to consider the Council of People's Commissars as the legitimate Russian government:

Cabinet—The President read speech & message of Trotsky, who said America entered war at behest of Wall Street and men whose property came through making munitions. Lansing thought T[rotsky] misguided but honest. . . . No answer now unless in message to Congress, for any answer would imply recognition. W[oodrow] W[ilson] said action of Lenine & Trotsky sounded like opera bouffe, talking of armistice with Germany when a child would know Germany would control & dominate & destroy any chance for the democracy they desire.[29]

Wilson appeared convinced that the Bolshevik policy served the interests of Russia's enemy, Germany. He applied his interpretation of the world war as a conflict between democracy and autocracy to the analysis of Russian policy. To Wilson, a separate Soviet peace treaty with Germany was not a reaction to the expansionist war aims of the Western European Allies, but a rejection of the democratic aims of the February Revolution. The president reduced the entire political development in Russia to the question of whether or not the new regime would stand for the same goals as the United States.

Wilson reiterated this opinion in the first public comment on the October Revolution on 12 November 1917 at the annual meeting of the American Federation of Labor in Buffalo. He called it "amazing" that any group of persons could be so "ill-informed as to suppose, as some groups in Russia apparently suppose, that any reforms planned in the interest of the people can live in the presence of a Germany powerful enough to undermine or overthrow them by intrigue or force." Any state that would agree to cooperate with the present German government was "compounding for its own destruction." Wilson repeated that the Soviet policy served German interests, a public statement well short of accusing them of deliberately conspiring with Germany. He believed that they refused to try to achieve a democratic peace for ideological reasons: "What I am opposed to is not the feeling of the pacifists, but their stupidity. . . . I want peace, but I know how to get it, and they don't."[30]

A peace treaty was now conceivable for Wilson only after the military defeat of Germany. Democratic peace negotiations could only be assumed after the threat of a German victory was over. He thereby replied to the Soviet ideological peace offensive with a moral argument. The Bolshevik propaganda led to a weakening of the democratic war party in Russia. That, in Wilson's eyes, proved that the coup d'état had brought a pro-German autocratic government into power there.

This interpretation of the revolution was questioned in December 1917 in an "Inquiry" report. The Inquiry was a semi-official committee of academics that had been formed on orders of Edward House in the fall of 1917. Its task was to make suggestions about the future European peace order.[31] The Inquiry was convinced that the radical Russian anticapitalism was more opposed to German imperialism than to Allied liberalism:

It is often overlooked that the Russian revolution, inspired as it is by deep hatred of autocracy, contains within it at least three other great motives of serious danger to German domination: 1) anti-capitalist feeling, which would be fully as intense, or more intense, against German capitalism; 2) a religious love of Russia . . . ; and 3) a powerful nationalist feeling among the Moderates, who will either return to power or at least exercise a strong influence in Russia. The revolution, therefore, must be regarded not only as inherently difficult for the Germans to manage and to muster, but as being in itself a great dissolving force through its sheer example.[32]

The Inquiry considered the liberalization of the Allied war aims a precondition of a change in the Russian attitude toward the Allies. Among Wilson's immediate advisers, only House shared the Inquiry's view that the Allies should prevent a breach in the anti-German alliance by modifying their war aims. On 30 November, while participating in a meeting of the Interallied Conference in Paris, House sent Wilson the draft of a resolution about war aims that read in part: "The Allies and the United States declare that they are not waging war for the purpose of aggression or indemnity. The sacrifices they are making are in order that militarism shall not continue to cast its shadow over the world, and that nations shall have the right to lead their lives in the way that seems to them best for the development of their general welfare." The following day, Wilson cabled House his general agreement with the draft of the resolution: "The resolution you suggest is entirely in line with my thought and has my approbation. . . . Our people and Congress will not fight for any selfish aims on the part of any belligerent with the possible exception of Alsace-Lorraine." Wilson's and House's views differed only in details. Wilson wrote concerning the Allied secret agreements about the division of the Balkans into spheres of influence: "Territorial aspirations must be left for decision of all, at Peace Conference especially plans for division of territory of such as have been contemplated in Asia Minor."[33]

From his conversations with British and French diplomats, House knew that the European Allies would not agree to any resolution that would question their claim to territorial gains from the war. In a cable to the president on 2 December, he expressed his disappointment with the British and French positions: "There have been long and frequent discussions as to Russia, but the result has not been satisfactory to me. I wanted a clear declaration along the lines of my cable to you of Friday. England passively was willing, France indifferently against it, Italy actively so."[34]

In House's eyes, the Allies were an obstacle to the intended liberalization of the war aims. He wrote in his diary in early December: "I wish I could say what I would really like to say [at the closing session of the Interallied Conference], but with the reactionary crowd I find here I do not dare to do so. More would be lost than could be gained."[35]

Wilson therefore faced a dilemma. He could continue to refer to the war as a democratic crusade and ignore the expansionist goals of the Allies. The Western democracies, including the United States, then would continue to be the target of Soviet propaganda. Alternatively, the president could insist on a modification of the war aims. That might cause frictions within the alliance and could endanger victory in the war over the Central Powers.[36]

To Wilson, maintaining unity among the Allies in the war against Imperial Germany had priority over ideological considerations about war aims. He refused to demand a commitment about the liberalization of their war aims from his alliance partners. Wilson's rhetoric, however, never displayed any doubt about the democratic basis of the peace for which the Allies were striving. In his State of the Union Address on 4 December 1917, a few days after the exchange of cables with House, Wilson again interpreted the war as a battle between democracy and autocracy. In that speech, "war aims" did not include questions about the future of individual European or colonial territories, but only the determination about whether the future political structure of Europe would be democratic:

I can not help thinking that if they [Allied war aims] had been made plain at the very outset [of the war] the sympathy and enthusiasm of the Russian people might have been once and for all enlisted on the side of the Allies. . . . Had they believed these things at the very moment of their revolution . . . the sad reverses which have marked the progress of their affairs towards an ordered and stable government of free men might have been avoided.[37]

Wilson stepped up his criticism of the Bolsheviks in response to their challenges. He accused them of deliberately deceiving the Russian people about the Allied war aims and about the nature of Bolshevik cooperation with Imperial Germany. "The Russian people," he continued, "have been poisoned by the very same false-hoods that have kept the German people in the dark, and the poison has been administered by the very same hands. The only possible antidote is the truth."[38] Wilson's statement implied a close connection between the Soviets and the Germans.

After the Allies had rejected a liberalization of their war aims, Wilson increased the pressure on the Bolsheviks because of their continued anti-Allied propaganda. During the following months, Wilson came to favor an alternative concept for a Russian policy which was conceived by Lansing. Diary entries and memoranda from early December on demonstrate his disdain for the Soviets. On 7 December, Lansing noted in his diary: "The correct policy for a government which believes in political institutions as they now exist and based on nationality and private property, is to leave these dangerous idealists alone and have no direct dealings with them." Only a few days later, however, in a letter to Wilson he suggested taking concrete steps against the Bolsheviks. His reflections about the Russian situation had led to the result "that the Bolsheviki are determined to prevent Russia from taking further part in the war." In a letter to Wilson from 2 January 1918, he expressed his concern that Trotsky's "presentation of peace terms may well appeal to the average man, who will not perceive the fundamental errors on which they are based." The addressee of the Soviet propaganda, Lansing continued, was the proletariat of every country. That presented a "very real danger in view of the present social unrest throughout the world." But the main flaw of the Soviet peace initiative was the overemphasis on the principle of national self-determination: "If the Bolsheviks intend to suggest that every community . . . can determine its allegiance to this or that political state or to become independent, the present political organization of the world would be shattered and the same disorder would generally prevail as now exists in Russia. It would be international anarchy."[39]

In this memorandum, written exclusively for the president, Lansing did not mention the possibility of a German conspiracy. His concern that the Soviet initiatives were designed to arouse proletarian and nationalistic revolts must have been shared in Germany and Austria-Hungary. Germany's strong working-class parties made that country politically vulnerable to socialist propaganda. In that interpretation, Trotsky's propaganda was not at all in the interest of the

German government. Lansing tended toward the conclusion that Lenin and Trotsky were not German agents: "Lenin might be acting entirely in Germany's interest, but I cannot make that belief harmonize with some things which he has done."⁴⁰ But the secretary of state did not reach the conclusion to support the Bolsheviks. He was afraid of the social consequences that the success of the Soviet experiment would have for the capitalist world.

Wilson agreed with the general outline of Lansing's views and began to express warnings about socialism. In January 1918, he shared the concern that the Bolshevik ideology as a combination of peace and social revolutionary propaganda could attract the American and Western European proletariat. Wilson expressed his reservations about Soviet propaganda in a conversation with the departing British ambassador to Washington, Sir Cecil Spring-Rice, on 3 January 1918. According to Spring-Rice's minutes of the conversation with the president, Wilson complained that in the United States "active [socialist] agitation was proceeding. It was too early yet to say with positive certainty how successful this agitation had been. But it was evident that if the appeal of the Bolsheviki was allowed to remain unanswered, if nothing were done to counteract it, the effect would be great and would increase." The Soviets had urged all countries to end the war immediately. The only legitimate basis for the future peace was the wish of the people: "They should be allowed to live their own lives according to their own will and under their own laws." Every people should decide for themselves whether they wanted to become independent. This far-reaching concept of national self-determination would have led to the sovereignty of countless small national groups which in 1918 were part of other countries. Wilson opposed the application of the principle of self-determination to all people. "Pushed to its extreme, the principle would mean the disruption of existing governments, to an undefinable extent." Wilson had adopted Lansing's main argument that a too far-reaching right to national self-determination would lead to international anarchy.⁴¹

Wilson did not suggest any concrete peace proposals in his conversation with Spring-Rice. He merely repeated his accusations against the Soviets. His own war-aims statements remained rather shapeless. He maintained that the American people "would not fight this war for private ends. . . . [T]heir object was a stable peace and they did not believe a stable peace could be based on aggression." But the president was aware that current American propaganda was insufficient, and he announced that "it might become necessary . . . to define even more clearly those objects for which America was waging war."[42]

It was not only Wilson who saw the necessity of specifying American war aims. In early January 1918, Ambassador Francis and Edgar Sisson urged the president to restate America's democratic and anti-imperialist war aims. Francis urged the president to state U.S. war goals briefly but bluntly: "Soviet government professes to think Allies will participate in negotiations but Allies will probably decline. When doing so President or yourself [Secretary Lansing] should address a communication to the Russian people explaining the declination in order to prevent Russia's falling into the arms of Germany."[43]

In a speech before Congress on 8 January 1918, Wilson presented the principles of his own "program of the world's peace." The centerpiece of this program were fourteen principles for a future liberal-democratic world order. The president himself had drafted the fourteen points on the basis of suggestions from the Inquiry. He had also consulted additional experts of his own choice in drafting the points concerning specific foreign countries. Point 6, which established principles for the future U.S. policy toward Russia, was drafted in cooperation with House and Boris A. Bakhmet'ev. Bakhmet'ev had been appointed Russian ambassador to the United States by the Provisional Government in July 1917. After the October Revolution, he had refused to acknowledge the Council of People's Commissars as the legitimate government. The State Department granted him permission to stay in the United States as head of the "Extraordinary Embassy from Russia."[44]

Wilson began his Fourteen Points speech with a reference to the German-Russian peace negotiations at Brest-Litovsk. The Central Powers, Wilson explained, had presented a peace proposal to the Soviet delegation which disregarded Russia's sovereignty and the wishes of the people: "the Central Empires were to keep every foot of territory their armed forces had occupied." On the other hand, Wilson applauded the Soviet insistence on open negotiations: "the Russian representatives have insisted, very justly, very wisely, and in the true spirit of modern democracy, that the conferences they have been holding with Teutonic and Turkish statesmen should be held with open, not closed doors."[45] For the first time since the October Revolution, Wilson characterized the Bolsheviki favorably and lauded their "wise" and "democratic" way of bargaining.

This passage of the speech has drawn criticism from conservative Western historians. George F. Kennan, for example, wrote: "Most striking in these passages of the speech is the unqualified approval and sympathy with which the President treats Soviet diplomacy in the Brest-Litovsk talks." Kennan continues: "The President identified the statements of the Soviet negotiators at Brest-Litovsk with the voice of the Russian people. Actually, the Bolshevik regime had no mandate from the people."[46]

Despite this positive presentation of the Bolshevik position, Wilson, of course, never considered them a democratic party. His conciliatory characterization has to be seen against the background of the deteriorating Russian-German relations in early January 1918. During the so-called first Brest-Litovsk crisis (late December 1917 through early January 1918), Wilson had reason to believe that the peace negotiations had been terminated. In early January, American newspapers carried reports about severe Russian-German friction. The *Washington Post*, for example, reported on 5 January that the German peace proposals "are considered by Trotzky, Lenine and their colleagues absolutely inadmissible, the objectionable factor being principally the Germans' refusal to remove military pressure from their occupied territories."[47] In his Fourteen Points speech Wilson said: "The negotiations have been broken off." If the president was convinced that the peace negotiations had failed because the peace proposals had proven incompatible, Wilson's characterization of the Bolsheviks is easily understandable. The United States had always refused to negotiate peace conditions with Imperial Germany. Now the Soviet leadership had belatedly reached the same conclusion.

In point 6, Wilson demonstrated the contrast between the German and the American policy toward Russia:

The evacuation of all Russian territory and such a settlement of all questions affecting Russia as will secure the best and freest cooperation of the other nations of the world in obtaining for her an unhampered and unembarrassed opportunity for the independent determination of her own political development and national policy and assure her of a sincere welcome into the society of free nations under institutions of her own choosing.[48]

Wilson assured the Russian people that the U.S. policy was to evacuate the Russian territory of all foreign occupational forces and to safeguard the Russian right of national self-determination. But point 6 remained vague concerning concrete political questions. For example, it was anything but clear in January 1918 which territories constituted Russia. On 1 (14) November 1917, the Soviet government had passed a decree that gave all non-Russian ethnic national groups within the former Russian Empire the right to secede.[49] Did Wilson consider Finland, which had proclaimed its independence in early January 1918, as part of the Russian territory? Some Western historians answer this question in the affirmative. Historian Claude Fike, for example, noted that Wilson assumed the role of a "protector of Russian interests" in his 8 January speech. The president "had come to identify [Russian interests] as keeping Russian territorial unity intact." The president's goal was to avoid as many changes as possible in the Russian status until a new regime would come to power which would truly represent the will of the Russian people. Wilson's view on national self-determination was very different from that of the Bolsheviks. He did not consider the dissolution of large multinational states as the centerpiece of the right of self-determination. To him it was a synonym for democracy.[50] It was of no importance how large a country was and how many nationalities it comprised. It was only important that all citizens could participate in the democratic process of determining the policy of that country. Wilson had the example of his own country in mind, which to him resembled the ideal of democratic self-determination despite its size and national heterogeneity.

In January 1918, the president avoided all expressions of open hostility toward the Bolsheviks, despite his ideological differences with them. The immediate goal of the Fourteen Points speech was to secure further Russian participation in the war by expressing friendship and the willingness to aid the country. The speech, therefore, was directed toward the Bolsheviks and toward the Russian people. Wilson hoped the Soviets might change their policy after their talks with the German government had failed, and he tried to convince the population of the Allies' war aims. The president asked the Russians to continue the war and at the same time tried to stress the political differences between the U.S. and the Soviet political system. Edward House, who was aware of these conflicting objectives, remarked to Bakhmet'ev that it did not make "any difference how the President resented Russia's action, the part of wisdom was to segregate her, as far as we were able, from Germany, and that could only be done by the broadest and friendliest expressions of sympathy and a promise of more substantial help."[51]

The Soviet leadership's reaction to the Fourteen Points speech was mixed. On 11 January, Sisson and Raymond Robins met with Lenin and showed him the text of the speech. Lenin agreed to publish the text in Russian newspapers, but he also asked his American visitors when the United States would recognize the Soviet government.[52]

The separate German-Soviet peace negotiations Wilson referred to in his Fourteen Points speech had their origins in an invitation Leon Trotsky, the Soviet commissar for foreign affairs, had issued to the ambassadors of the Entente and Central Powers of 9 (22) November 1917. The Allied ambassadors decided in the afternoon of the same day to recommend to their governments that they should not reply to the invitation because the Soviet government was established by force and was not recognized by the Russian people. Two days later, on 11 (24) November, Trotsky issued a second invitation for a "general and not separate armistice." At the same time, he threatened to continue his appeals to the people of the Allied states if they refused to enter into negotiations. Western representatives in Russia recognized Trotsky's goal of embarrassing their governments. The Soviet commissar's second note, Francis cabled to the State Department on 28 November, was "insulting to Allied governments. It threatens appeals to peoples of countries whose Governments will not recognize him or refuse armistice and peace."[53]

In contrast to the Allies, the Imperial German government agreed to enter into immediate armistice negotiations with the Soviets. The talks commenced on 20 November (3 December) in Brest-Litovsk, the headquarters of the Eastern German armies. The armistice negotiations were successfully completed on 2 (15) December. A week later, talks aimed at reaching a peace treaty began. Those talks, in contrast, proved to be extremely difficult because the Soviets proposed a peace plan designed as a revolutionary model treaty to end World War I similar to Wilson's "peace without victory" proposals. On the first day of the negotiations, the Soviet delegation presented a six-point program that was based on the principles of the *Decree on Peace*. It demanded the complete withdrawal of all German military forces from areas occupied during the war as part of its call for a nonannexationist peace. Countries that had lost their independence during the conflict were to be restored as sovereign states. National groups that were not organized as sovereign states prior to the war would be free to decide whether they would become independent or whether they would join another country. No reparations payments should be demanded.[54]

An acceptance of these Soviet proposals would have made the entire German war-aims policy obsolete. The German army would have been forced to leave Courland, Lithuania, Poland, and the Ukraine despite the collapse of the Russian defense. The German Military High Command never seriously considered accepting those proposals, and through its delegation presented a program of its own that included the German annexation of those areas. Disillusioned about the chances of reaching a peace treaty without annexations, the Soviet delegation left Brest-Litovsk in late December. During this first Brest-Litovsk crisis, it seemed doubtful whether the talks would ever resume. The leadership of the Bolshevik party was split over the future course of the war policy. Lenin advocated a policy of immediate peace at all cost, but his view that a revolutionary war was not a practical option for the Bolsheviks was in a minority position.[55]

On 8 January 1918, the day Wilson gave the Fourteen Points speech, Trotsky left Petrograd to resume the Brest-Litovsk peace talks. The Soviet delegation had altered its tactics in negotiating with the Germans. Trotsky knew that Germany would not agree with his ideas about a peace without annexations. Therefore, he now started to use the meetings of the delegations, whose minutes were published, for propaganda purposes. He openly agitated for the proletarian revolution among the German soldiers. At the same time, progress of the negotiations was stalemated by Trotsky's unwillingness to respond to specific German peace proposals. In mid-January, German Foreign Minister Richard von Kühlmann, who headed the German delegation, demanded that the Soviets either accept or refuse the German offer. Trotsky was desperate. His hope that the presence of a high-ranking Soviet delegation at a

German military camp would lead to army mutinies and popular demands for an immediate peace had not materialized.

The Central Committee of the Bolshevik party remained divided about the question of a separate peace. A number of prominent party members, among them Nikolai Bukharin, pleaded for the immediate proclamation of a proletarian-revolutionary war. Lenin, on the other hand, still favored accepting the German proposals and endorsed the immediate conclusion of a separate peace. Trotsky's position was between those of Lenin and Bukharin. He wanted to inform the German delegation that Russia considered the war terminated but would refuse to sign a peace treaty dictated by Germany. On 14 (27) January 1918, the Third All-Russian Soviet Congress outvoted Lenin's appeal for accepting the German conditions and adopted Trotsky's "neither war nor peace" formula.[56]

On 27 January (10 February), the Soviet delegation informed the Germans of that decision. Immediately after the German-Russian armistice agreement expired on 17 February, the *Reichswehr* resumed fighting. The invading troops advanced without noticeable Russian resistance. Petrograd was threatened. The Central Committee realized the hopelessness of the situation and accepted new and much harsher German peace proposals unconditionally. The peace treaty was signed in Brest-Litovsk on 3 March 1918.[57] Under the treaty, Russia lost almost a quarter of its European territory that included some of the most productive agricultural areas, a third of its textile industry, and a quarter of its heavy industry.

The Soviet peace strategy immediately following the October Revolution was narrowly focused on the expectation of revolutionary upheavals in other countries. When those revolutions failed to materialize, the Soviets realized that their only alternative was accepting or rejecting Imperial Germany's conditions to end the war. By late February, sufficiently disillusioned about the prospect of a world revolution, the Soviets accepted Lenin's cautious course of foreign policy and actively sought aid from the capitalist Entente states. The Bolsheviks, historian Isaac Deutscher wrote, "began to wonder whether the road to peace would lead through revolution or whether, on the contrary, the road to revolution did not lead through peace." In the second case, the Soviets would for some time have to live side by side with capitalist states.[58]

The German-Russian antagonism which became apparent in January and February 1918 during the second Brest-Litovsk crisis aroused the interest of Allied diplomats in Russia. A few days before the German attack on the Eastern front, Ambassador Francis cabled to the State Department that he still believed in the "agent theory" but "recent events demonstrate they [Bolsheviki] did their work too well and were making inroads in Germany and Austria." The resumption of the war completely contradicted the view of a Soviet-German conspiracy that was underlying the Allied policy toward Russia. In a memorandum to the Supreme War Council on 27 February, Colonel James A. Ruggles, the American military attaché in Russia, described how "panic-stricken" Russian troops were leaving areas threatened by Germans in "large numbers by every means possible," and that Lenin and Trotsky had apparently offered their resignation.[59]

For a while it appeared that the Wilson administration might be willing to cooperate with the Soviets. In mid-January, Secretary Lansing showed Wilson a telegram from the chargé of the U.S. embassy in Copenhagen, Ulysses Grant-Smith. In this cable, Grant-Smith suggested that one of the Allies should grant the Bolsheviks diplomatic recognition as a "first practical step towards combating German intrigue in Russia." Recognition would facilitate communications with the de facto Russian government and could counteract German influence there. In a memorandum for Lansing about this suggestion, Wilson noted on 20 January: "Here is the ever-recurring question, How shall we deal with the Bolsheviki? This particular suggestion seems to me to have something in it worth considering, and I am writing to ask what your own view is."[60] But by that time Lansing had decided to pursue an anti-Bolshevik policy, and he refused to grant the Soviet government diplomatic recognition.

In early March, following the resumption of German hostilities on the Eastern front, Francis, too, began advocating conditional recognition of the Soviets if the fighting in Russia would continue. Leon Trotsky had approached Francis and asked what kind of support the Allies would grant Russia in case of a continuation of the war. Francis promised to support the Soviet wish for moral and material aid: "I have instructed military attache," Francis cabled to Secretary Lansing, "to assure Soviet government that I will recommend moral and material cooperation provided organized resistance is sincerely established which will give promise of retarding

German advance and engaging attention of troops who would otherwise be sent [to the] western front."61

But Wilson was not prepared to grant the Soviets any kind of support. He transmitted his reply to Trotsky's question in a note entitled "To the Russian People." It stated that "[t]he Government of the United States is unhappily not now in a position to render the direct and effective aid it would wish to render." The president again saw the conflict between democracy and autocracy as paramount to all other problems: "The whole heart of the people of the United States is with the people of Russia in the attempt to free themselves forever from autocratic government and become the masters of their own life." Addressing the note to the Russian people indicated that he considered both the Bolsheviks and the German government as autocratic rulers.62

On 1 (15) March 1918, the Fourth All-Russian Congress of Soviets ratified the peace treaty of Brest-Litovsk. Russia left the war alliance against the Central Powers. The end of Russia's participation in the war, however, was far from what the Bolsheviks had initially hoped for by issuing the *Decree on Peace*. Instead of ending the war with the socialist revolutionary governments of Germany and France, modeled after the Soviet example, the Bolsheviks signed a humiliating treaty with Imperial Germany that testified to the military weakness, political isolation, and ideological frustration of the Soviets. The German advance in mid-February had shown that Russian troops were unable to stop the invading forces. The Bolsheviks' hope of a world revolution appeared to be an illusion for the time being.63

After the October Revolution, Wilson immediately perceived the Soviet revolutionaries as ideological opponents. Their ideas about socialist dictatorships and public ownership of the means of production were contrary to Wilson's political goals. Soviet military decisions between November 1917 and March 1918 increased Wilson's discontent with the new Russian regime. The Soviets concluded a separate peace treaty with the Imperial German government and justified their action with ideological rhetoric. They even charged that the American interests in the war were economic rather than liberal-democratic. Wilson's reaction demonstrated his uncertainty about the nature of the Soviet challenge. He appeared to believe that the Bolsheviks acted in accordance with German orders and yet encouraged socialist uprisings there.

Lansing and the other presidential advisers disregarded those inconsistencies in favor of an anti-Bolshevik policy. It wasn't until the spring of 1918 that the Wilson administration began to think about actively intervening in Russia.

3

The Decision to Intervene

Mr. Wilson . . . should be judged by what he was and did prior to August 4, 1918, the date of the paper justifying the attack on Russia. That was the first of his acts which was unlike him; and I am sure the beginning of the sad end.
— Louis D. Brandeis, 11 May 1924[1]

After the October Revolution, the Wilson administration faced the dilemma of trying to ensure continued Russian participation in the war, while at the same time wanting to have as little contact with the Bolsheviks as possible. In March 1918, that policy proved to be futile when Russia left the war. "Viewed through Western eyes," one historian noted, the Soviet decision to sign a separate agreement with Imperial Germany was "nothing short of disaster." Germany was free to relocate substantial numbers of troops to the Western front long before the American Expeditionary Force had reached its full strength. Faced with that threat on the Western front, Allied politicians debated plans to keep German troops engaged in Russia either by revitalizing the Russian war efforts or, if necessary, by overthrowing the Bolsheviks and supporting a Russian civil war faction that favored continued participation in the war. Persistent demands by the British and French governments for Wilson to join an intervention in Russia finally met with the president's approval in July 1918. He agreed to send American troops to Russia for the stated reason of preventing the Germans from utilizing war materials stored in Russia. Just as important for him, however, was maintaining Allied unity during the decisive period of the world war.[2]

American representatives in Russia recommended against the United States entering into official diplomatic relations with the Soviet regime immediately after the October Revolution. "I consider it unwise to recognize the *de facto* government of the Bolsheviki," Arthur Bullard, head of the Russian Office of the Committee on Public Information wrote on 27 November 1917. In "sharp contrast to the revolution of March," he continued, the overthrow of the Provisional Government in October was a "minority insurrection." On 1 December, the State Department officially decided not to enter into official relations with the Soviet government and ordered Ambassador Francis in Petrograd that he was "to make no reply to [Soviet] communications" and informed him that the administration "awaits further developments." In his *War Memoirs*, Secretary of State Robert Lansing later noted that "from this time on the policy of non-recognition of the Bolsheviks was pursued without variation."[3] The Wilson administration continued to consider the Provisional Government as the legal government of Russia, but was nevertheless interested in learning about events in Soviet Russia.

Despite the orders given to Francis not to engage in official diplomatic dealings with the Soviets, the State Department maintained its ambassadorial and consular staff in Russia. Francis justified his remaining in a country whose government he did not recognize by pointing out that he was not accredited to any government, but to the Russian people. "I will not leave Russia until I am compelled to do so by force. My government and the American people are too deeply interested in the welfare of the Russian people to leave Russia." The State Department's real interest in maintaining an embassy in Russia was more prosaic. The embassy staff was the only group of well-qualified observers that could gather much needed information about political and military developments in Russia. On 15 December, for example, the State Department advised Consul General Maddin Summers in Moscow to "keep in close touch with developments in Moscow and Moscow district."[4]

While official government representatives remained in Russia for the purpose of gathering general information, the administration maintained contact with the Soviet leadership through American citizens residing in Petrograd on official, but not governmental, business. The American embassy used the services of Raymond Robins, the chairman of a commission of the American Red Cross in Petrograd from December 1917 until May 1918, for contacts with Lenin and Trotsky. Francis described Robins's activities in countless cables to the State Department. On 21 January 1918, for example, he wrote that "Robins, Sisson, especially former, in close relations with Smolny [seat of Soviet government]. Robins visits me daily, gives desired information concerning Bolshevik policies."[5]

The administration's difficulties in pursuing the two interests of gathering information about the Soviets, but at the same time avoiding official recognition of the regime, became obvious when the State Department ordered the military attaché of the Petrograd embassy, General William V. Judson, a member of the earlier Root mission to Russia, to terminate his contacts with Trotsky. Judson had tried to establish personal contacts with leading Bolsheviks immediately after the revolution. His goal was to accommodate the Soviets' material needs as much as possible to prevent the conclusion of a separate Russo-German peace treaty. During a conversation with Trotsky on 1 December 1917 in the Soviet foreign commisar's official residence, Judson suggested that the Soviet government should only enter into armistice negotiations, but should refuse to talk about a peace treaty with the German negotiators. Judson's main objective was to prevent the *Reichswehr* from relocating large forces from the Eastern to the Western front. As long as Russia had not concluded a peace treaty, Germany presumably would be hesitant to order such a shift in its troop deployment.[6]

The following day, the Soviet newspaper *Izvestiya* carried an account of the conference. The article, written by Trotsky himself, stated that Judson had made it clear at the outset of their meeting that he could not speak in the name of the United States government because Washington had not recognized the Soviet government. The ambassadors of the Western European Allies nevertheless considered Judson's visit to Trotsky as a first step toward granting the Soviets diplomatic recognition and protested against Judson's contacts in a letter to Francis. The State Department in Washington received information about the 1 December meeting only after it had taken place. Lansing joined those who criticized the meeting and repeated his order to the Petrograd embassy to "withhold all direct communication with Bolshevik government." The State Department decided against further meetings between Judson and the Soviets, though Trotsky had offered an opportunity to prevent, or at least delay, a major relocation of German troops to the Western front. But accepting Trotsky's proposal would have implied the need for cooperation with the Bolsheviks; Wilson and Lansing were not prepared to enter into relations with them.[7]

Secretary Lansing not only categorically refused to cooperate with the Bolsheviks, but he also thought about ways of how to end their regime. On 12 December, he presented a memorandum to Wilson, drafted jointly with Secretary of the Treasury William G. McAdoo, in which they explored the possibilities of an overthrow of the Soviet government. Lansing and McAdoo expressed their belief that the anti-Bolshevik Generals Aleksei M. Kaledin and Lavr' G. Kornilov would be able to take over power in Russia. A necessary precondition to this overthrow, however, would be substantial material help from abroad, which had to be provided secretly. "It would seem unwise for this government to supply openly Kaledine and his party because of the attitude which it seems advisable to take with the Petrograd authorities but it is felt that the Kaledine group should be shown that the Allied governments are most sympathetic with his efforts." Under the law, the authors continued, it would be illegal to grant the Russian counter-revolutionaries financial assistance. Money could only be spent on recognized governments. None of the anti-Bolshevik factions, however, could presently be considered fulfilling governmental requirements: "Without actually recognizing his [Kaledin's] groups as a de facto government, which is at present impossible since it has not taken form, this government cannot under the law loan money to them." Instead, Lansing and McAdoo suggested: "The only practicable cause seems to be for the British and French Government to finance the Kaledine enterprise in so far as it is necessary, and for this government to loan them the money to do so."[8]

Lansing and McAdoo advocated a policy of interfering in the internal affairs of Russia. Their goal was to finance and direct an anti-Soviet counterrevolution. The decision to support General Lavr' Kornilov also indicated the kind of policy Lansing hoped to revitalize in Russia. Kornilov had first achieved notoriety when he attempted to overthrow the Provisional Government in September 1917. He justified his abortive coup attempt with the argument that the government was too soft on the Soviets and did not pursue the war vigorously enough. On 27 August (9 September) 1917, Kornilov announced that he would increase the Russian military efforts if he could take over power.[9] The coup attempt of early September, however, failed and united Prime Minister Kerensky and the Bolsheviks in their fight against the insurrection. After his defeat, Kornilov retreated southward in an attempt to gather new forces where he still remained at the end of the year.

Wilson examined Lansing's and McAdoo's suggestion to support Kornilov on 12 December and added to the memorandum: "This has my entire approval." On 16 December, De Witt Clinton Poole, a member of the staff of the American Consulate General in Moscow, traveled to Rostov-on-the-Don to establish contacts with anti-Bolshevik military forces there. After conversations with Generals Kaledin, Mikhail Alekseev, and the former Russian Foreign Minister Miliukov, Poole on 23 December advocated granting the anti-Soviet movements in southern Russia financial support.[10]

Poole's hope to supply Kaledin for an attack on the Soviet government appears to have been wishful thinking. Poole's estimates as to the numbers of troops Kaledin commanded must have aroused doubts in Washington. He believed that Kaledin's army consisted of 1,500 to 2,000 soldiers. In the winter of 1917/18, Kaledin lost a considerable number of his troops through desertion. By early February 1918, his position had deteriorated so badly that he committed suicide.[11]

The governments in London and Paris urged the Wilson administration to take part in an even more far-reaching military intervention in Russia. The Western European Allies were even more concerned about the separate German-Russian peace negotiations than the United States. A relocation of German troops to the Western front would have intensified the fighting on French soil. The French government, therefore, advocated active support of anti-Bolshevik forces and ultimately the installation of a pro-Allied government in Petrograd. The French ambassador to Washington, Jules J. Jusserand, suggested on 8 January 1918 that the State Department take "some joint action tending to protect, if possible, Siberia from Maximalist contagion." He continued: "This would offer a chance to prevent German influence, which in the event of a separate peace might predominate in northern Russia, from getting foothold in Vladivostok to the great detriment of the situation of the Allies in the Far East."[12] To the French government it appeared clear that Germany was the main beneficiary of the Bolshevik takeover in Russia and Siberia.

The Bolsheviks were able to seize power in most Russian cities by the end of 1917. They were less successful in rural areas of northern and southern Russia, and in Siberia. In those areas, Bolshevik propaganda and military units faced small but well-equipped and determined resistance groups. In early January 1918, the Allies were particularly concerned about whether the Bolsheviks could seize power in the coastal cities of Archangel, Murmansk, and Vladivostok because huge amounts of war matériel that had been delivered to Russia prior to the October Revolution was stored in these ports in the winter of 1917/18. The collapse of the Russian railway system had made the transport of matériel to the front impossible. The British under secretary for foreign affairs, Lord Robert Cecil, estimated in January 1918 that there were 648,000 tons of material stored in Vladivostok alone.[13]

In mid-January the State Department informed Jusserand that it did not share his concern about the political development in Siberia: "The American Government is disposed to believe that such a military mission as is proposed [to protect allied stores in Vladivostok] is not required by the present condition of affairs in Siberia." Lansing did not deny the threat of a Bolshevik takeover in Siberia. But he also believed that any kind of direct foreign military intervention there would lead to greater popular support for the Bolsheviks: "It is believed that it would be likely to offend those Russians who are now in sympathy with the aims and desires which the United States and its cobelligerents have at heart in making war and might result in assisting all factions in Siberia against them."[14]

The popular reaction to an intervention was only one of the problems Lansing expected. Another critical issue was geography. American, British, and French troops were engaged in a war in

Western Europe. Relocating substantial troops to Vladivostok would have been a logistical and military challenge during the war. The British and French governments therefore wanted to encourage Japan to provide the bulk of the troops to invade Vladivostok. The goal of the intervention was to prevent the military supply from falling into the hands of the Bolsheviks. The British War Office and the French army command agreed in early February 1918 upon an intervention plan in Russia with Japanese participation. On 19 February the Supreme War Council, which coordinated all Allied military action in the war, cabled to the State Department that a Japanese intervention in Siberia was advisable. A Japanese intervention in Siberia that would include taking possession of the Trans-Siberian Railway from Vladivostok to the city of Chelyabinsk in the Ural Mountains would reinforce the "national element in Russia and Siberia to the detriment of the forces of anarchy" and would "prevent the Germans from withdrawing their troops to the western front." The war council dismissed the argument that a foreign intervention would cause a popular uproar: The "orderly elements" in Russia and Siberia demanded an "energetic intervention" and all classes of Russian society have appealed for a Japanese intervention, many Russian officers "having even asked to serve with the invading Japanese forces."[15]

When Wilson learned about the Allied plans for a Japanese intervention in Siberia, he did not express any objections on grounds of principle. He only hoped that prior to taking any military action on Russian soil the government in Tokyo would promise not to seek its own advantage. When asked at the cabinet meeting of 1 March 1918 whether the United States should aid Japan in its invasion, Wilson answered:

"No," for the very practical reason that we had no ships. We had difficulty in providing for our men in France and for our Allies. . . . How hopeless it would be to carry everything seven or eight thousand miles—not only men and munitions, but food! . . . Yes, we were needed—perhaps as a guarantee of good faith on Japan's part that she would not go too far, nor stay too long. But we would not do it. And besides, Russia would not like it, therefore we must keep hands off and let Japan take the blame and the responsibility.[16]

Wilson told Lansing to inform the Allied ambassadors in Washington that the United States government had no objections to

Japanese intervention in Siberia, but that it could not participate with its own forces.[17]

Wilson's acceptance of plans for a Japanese invasion drew considerable criticism in Washington both from opponents of the Bolshevik regime and from advocates of better American-Soviet relations. Edward House conferred about this problem with Elihu Root and Boris Bakhmet'ev on 2 and 3 March. Afterward House wrote in a memorandum to Wilson that Root "thinks that even if Japan should announce her purpose to retire when the war was over . . . the racial dislike which the Russians have for the Japanese would throw Russia into arms of Germany." Bakhmet'ev, the ambassador of the Russian Provisional Government, was "of a like opinion." House summarized the results of his conversation: "We are treading upon exceedingly delicate and dangerous ground, and are likely to lose that fine moral position you have given the Entente cause." The American position will "not be better than that of Germany."[18]

On 5 March, Wilson reversed his attitude toward a Japanese intervention in Siberia. In a note to the government in Tokyo, he questioned the "wisdom" of a military action in Russia. If Japan should continue its invasion plans, Washington expected written assurances that they would be exclusively in "Russia's interest, and with the sole view of holding it safe against Germany." Otherwise, he believed, "the Central powers could and would make it appear that Japan was doing in the East exactly what Germany is doing in the West." Under Secretary of State Frank Polk commented on Wilson's change of mind in a note to Lansing, saying that it was a change of position, but "I do not know that it will materially effect the situation. . . . [Y]ou will probably see what influenced him, namely the position of this Government in the eyes of the democratic people of the world."[19] Polk correctly pointed out Wilson's desire to fulfill the highest moral and democratic standards with his policy decisions. The problem, however, was that those standards brought his policy in conflict with America's Allies.

Great Britain and France continued to favor a Japanese intervention in Siberia. The government in Tokyo, however, refused to intervene on the Russian mainland unless Washington publicly welcomed such a step and pledged financial support for the invasion. Japanese Foreign Minister Ichiro Motono informed the British ambassador to Japan, Sir William Conyngham Greene, on

7 March that "unless the Allies could count on the President's support it would perhaps be better that action should be deferred."[20]

The governments in London and Paris disagreed with Wilson and attempted to win Washington's agreement to an intervention. British Foreign Minister Arthur Balfour sent a note to Wilson on 18 March that stated: "What Germany desires is that Russia should be impotent during the war, subservient after it, and in the meantime to supply food and raw material to Central Powers." In Balfour's analysis, Russia was not "out of the war" after the separate peace with Germany but continued to provide the Central Powers with essential raw materials and food. An intervention in Russia, therefore, served the needs of the democratic elements in Russia and helped the Allied war efforts. Balfour considered Japan to be the only power able to fight German dominance in Russia in the immediate future and urged Wilson to revise his rejection of the Japanese intervention. "Japan is in a position to do much more in Siberia than France Italy America and Britain can possibly do in Murmansk or Archangel."[21]

Wilson, however, in a conversation with the British ambassador to Washington, Lord Reading, on 19 March, reaffirmed his opposition to a Japanese intervention. Wilson, as Reading cabled to London, did not believe that a Japanese intervention would make such an impression on Germany "as to cause German troops to be withdrawn from the Western front." Reading noted: "The President much regretted that America should be standing out against the views of the Allies on this question. He felt the force of the argument that the Americans would cause disappointment to the Allies but he could not think that the situation here was completely understood by them."[22] Wilson felt a moral pressure to reach an agreement with the Allies, but he interpreted the situation differently. It was only in late May that Wilson began to reconcile his ideological opposition to an intervention in general and a Japanese intervention in particular with the need to cooperate with the Allies.

Wilson based his rejection of a Japanese or joint Allied intervention on a large number of memoranda written in early 1918. The supreme commander of the American Pacific Fleet, Admiral Austin M. Knight, for example, wrote in a report to the president that "[i]t is universally believed by Russians that Japan desires to take over a large part of Siberia." But Knight's main argument against the intervention was that the German army was not able to seize the stocks of weapons and ammunition in Vladivostok because it was "scattered in armories over many miles, making it impracticable to guard all sections efficiently but . . . for the same reasons it is impossible that any great quantity could be destroyed. . . . There is, moreover, absolutely no danger at present that munitions now here (Vladivostok) will reach the Germans." Knight continued: "It is safe to say that no real necessity exists for armed intervention in Siberia unless intervention is desirable for the establishment of law and order."[23]

Basil Miles, the State Department's Russian expert, also warned against intervention by the Japanese. The Russians "have an in-grained suspicion and hostile feeling toward the Japanese. . . . The Russian peasants and the proletariat have not yet got to the point where they want any uninvited help from the outside."[24] An invasion, Miles contended, should not be conducted by Japan alone. It would also be advisable to seek an invitation to intervention from a Russian party, and this possibility was discussed over the next few weeks.

The first request for an intervention came, to the Allies' surprise, from the Bolsheviks. In mid-March Leon Trotsky, who was forming the Red Army, requested that officers be sent to Russia to help instruct the new Russian troops. Trotsky's offer was the first in a series of diplomatic initiatives designed to cooperate with the West and to counteract the anti-Bolshevik attitudes in the Allied capitals.[25]

Trotsky's suggestion was received favorably by the French government. In a memorandum of 8 April, the government in Paris noted that the "Maximalists themselves might be induced to accept the Japanese intervention which the Ambassadors admit is necessary to combat Germany and make a reorganization of Russia possible." The Soviets' willingness to accept Allied support in building a new Russian army could be understood as the beginning of a new Soviet attitude toward the West. The French government suggested a double strategy to react to Trotsky's suggestion. First, the Bolshevik invitation for cooperation should be accepted. Second, however, the Allies should maintain their simultaneous contacts with the counterrevolutionary armies to fight the Bolsheviks if necessary: "Japanese intervention is more than ever necessary to combat Germany. . . . [I]t will only work its full effect if it bears the character of an inter-allied participation and if the Bolshevik Government is prevailed on to accept it. . . . [A]llied personalities who have access to Trotsky are under the impression that he could probably be induced to accept Japanese intervention." The author believed that should this strategy fail, "a Siberian Government which would restore order with the desired help of Japanese troops could easily be constituted."[26]

In the spring of 1918, the State Department received countless reports about the founding of anti-Bolshevik organizations in Russia. On 12 April, for example, the American consul in Harbin (China), Charles K. Moser, introduced the Siberian Regional Government to the State Department. It consisted of members of the former Constituent Assembly that had been forcefully dissolved by the Bolsheviks in January. The Regional Government's political goal was to secure "the establishment of law and order" and to fight the Bolsheviks on behalf of the "legal imperial authority of the All-Russian Constituent Assembly." Furthermore, the government's goal was to protect the territorial integrity of Siberia, to convene an All-Siberian Constituent Assembly, and to join the Allies in actively combating the "Bolshevik-German peace in order to conclude a universal democratic peace."[27]

After his rejection of the Allied proposal to intervene in Siberia in early March, Wilson was confronted with growing pressure from the Allies to participate in an intervention or to cooperate with one of the counterrevolutionary factions in the Russian civil war. The president did not support any of the alternatives wholeheartedly. He had questioned the legal and moral justification of intervention on countless occasions. Political and military advisers had warned him against publicly endorsing a Japanese attack on Siberia. If the government in Tokyo would follow an imperialist policy there, the United States would be blamed. At the same time, Allied pressure for intervention grew and Wilson's resistance weakened. The president never considered the option of military cooperation with the Bolsheviks. There are no documents from the spring of 1918 that contain any indication that he had softened his negative attitude toward the Soviets. A cooperation with them was incompatible with his ideological expectation of a victory of democratic liberalism over socialism. Wilson could not give up his policy of nonintercourse with the Soviets while the truly democratic forces in Russia were fighting the Bolsheviks. Slowly, Wilson began considering the opposite policy. In mid-April, for the first time he expressed genuine interest in learning about the Russian counter-revolutionary movements. On 18 April he advised Secretary Lansing: "I would very much value a memorandum containing *all* that we know about these *nuclei* of self-governing authority that seem to be springing up in Siberia. It would afford me a great deal of satisfaction to get behind the most nearly representative of them, if it can indeed draw leadership and control to itself."[28]

The State Department presented Wilson with the latest findings about anti-Bolshevik movements in two memoranda of 12 April and 22 May 1918. In the first of those memoranda, Basil Miles listed the various movements known to the State Department. In another report one month later, Miles went a step further and recommended granting U.S. assistance to two antirevolutionary groups. Miles considered General Grigori Semenoff's movement particularly promising. Semenoff had increased the size of his army from 700 to 2,500 men and was currently in control of the crossing point of the Amur and Trans-Siberian Railways. "Semenoff's policy is to keep the Siberian Railway open and overthrow the Bolsheviki. He is variously reported as a liberal and as a reactionary; the former appears to be nearer the fact." If the president should decide to lend aid to Semenoff, Miles recommended that he should also support the Czechoslovak troops in Russia. Miles estimated that there were about 6,000 Czechoslovak soldiers in Vladivostok and another 90,000 in western Siberia.[29]

Those Czechoslovak troops had fought in the world war as part of the Russian army. At the outset of the conflict in the summer of 1914, Czechs and Slovaks living in Russia were gathered in special units that grew to 45,000 to 60,000 men during the war by incorporating Slavic soldiers who had deserted the Austrian army. Their main goal in the war was to gain independence from Austria and establish a sovereign Czechoslovak state. The treaty of Brest-Litovsk which ended the war on the Eastern front did not make any provisions about Slavic independence from the Habsburg Empire. The Czech soldiers, therefore, strove to continue the war against Germany. In December 1917, the French government assumed supreme command over the Czechoslovak troops and ordered them to travel to France to serve on the Western front. An overland transport of the soldiers from Russia to France was impossible during the war. The only solution was to provide a sea passage for them via Archangel in northern Russia or Vladivostok in Siberia. The Soviet government, too, was interested in an immediate transport of these armed and hostile troops from its soil, and on 14 March 1918 ordered the passage through Vladivostok because the northern harbor of Archangel was still icebound in the spring of 1918.[30]

On the transport from the Ukraine to eastern Siberia, a number of confrontations occurred between the Czechs and local Soviet authorities. On 21 March, for example, the Omsk Soviet prohibited the transport of the Czechs eastward because it had not been informed about their relocation. The misunderstanding was solved only after five days. The Czechs believed that the Soviets deliberately slowed down their departure to prevent their participation in the war on the Western front. The Soviet government, on the other hand, faced the problem of transporting tens of thousands of Czech soldiers eastward on the single-track Trans-Siberian Railroad, while at the same time (mid-April 1918) the German government insisted on the immediate repatriation of German prisoners of war from eastern Siberian prison camps.[31]

After a revolt of Czech troops against a local Soviet in the Ural Mountains, Trotsky ordered the immediate disarmament of the Czech units. The Czechs refused to obey this order and continued their march eastward. By late June, about 15,000 of them had reached Vladivostok and were waiting for ships to take them to France. The rest of the troops at that time were still in the Irkutsk region.

By early summer, the Czechs' refusal to hand over their arms developed into a controversy about the future of the Bolshevik rule in Siberia. Local anti-Soviet groups joined the Czechs' fight. In Vladivostok, the Czechs asked Allied representatives for weapons to support their compatriots still fighting along the Trans-Siberian Railway. The American consul to Vladivostok, John K. Caldwell, cabled to Washington on 25 June that the "[e]stablishment of anti-Bolshevik Siberian government [appeared] probable. The government genuinely eager to resume hostilities against Germany. Czech total 50,000: 15,000, Vladivostok." This force, he went on, was a "splendid adequate nucleus for new Siberian army." The American representative to China, Paul S. Reinsch, cabled the State Department: "All American representatives in Siberia are agreed that Allied intervention is absolutely demanded. Siberia will be in

German control unless immediate action is taken. Joint action desirable because of Russian fear of Japan. Presence of Czecho-Slovaks can be utilized. American force of 10,000 considered sufficient." Secretary Lansing recommended on 23 June using the Czechs as a "nucleus for military occupation of the Siberian railway." On 3 July, the Supreme War Council in Paris joined the demand "to bring assistance to the Czech forces."[32] All democratic elements would welcome Western support for the Czechs: "There is much evidence . . . that the best liberal and democratic elements in Russia . . . are animated partly by disgust with the autocratic methods of the Bolsheviks, partly by the determination not to submit to the humiliation . . . of the Brest-Litovsk treaties."

In late spring and early summer, Wilson's attitude toward intervention shifted slowly from a wholly negative attitude to one advocating a limited military action in Russia. In late May he told the British intelligence officer William Wiseman that if large U.S. and British forces were placed along the Trans-Siberian Railroad, the Russian people would assist in the defense of their country.[33]

On 6 July, Wilson again discussed the Allied plan for intervention with Secretary Lansing, Secretary of War Newton B. Baker, Secretary of the Navy Josephus Daniels, and with military officers. In the course of these discussions it became apparent that the president still rejected the idea of reestablishing the Eastern front after an intervention in Russia: "The establishment of an eastern front through a military expedition, even if it was wise to employ a large Japanese force, is physically impossible." The view in July 1918 that the intervention would not serve the paramount goal of victory over Germany did not lead to the outright rejection of the idea of intervention. Wilson was now willing to send troops to Russia to aid the Czechoslovaks: "The present situation of the Czecho-Slovaks requires this government and other governments to make an effort to aid those at Vladivostok in forming a junction with their compatriots in western Siberia." The president defined a limited goal which the United States would try to achieve in the Far East. The Czechoslovak soldiers that were still in central Siberia should be joined with their countrymen in Vladivostok. Wilson and his advisers agreed to a three-point program: (1) the United States and Japan would deliver to the Czechs hand weapons and ammunition, (2) Washington and Tokyo would each dispatch 7,000 soldiers to Siberia to secure safe passage for the Czechs on the Trans-Siberian

Railway, and (3) Allied and Czech troops would establish a joint government in Vladivostok.[34]

Wilson presented his position on military action in Russia to the Allies in a note on 17 July 1918. In it he emphasized that the administration viewed intervention strictly as a means of fighting Germany: "The controlling purpose of the Government of the United States is to do everything that is necessary and effective to win [the war]." The administration agreed to send a limited military contingent to Russia because the Supreme War Council believed this to be a valuable contribution to the general war effort. Wilson rejected the idea of an intervention in Russia that would only add to the confusion there and injure rather than help the country. He only saw the need of a limited "military action" to help the Czechoslovaks consolidate their forces and to "get into successful cooperation with their Slavic kinsmen and to steady any efforts at self-governance or self-defence in which the Russians themselves may be willing to accept assistance." Wilson emphasized that he did not plan to interfere in Russia's internal affairs. None of the Allied governments, he wrote, should contemplate interference of any kind with either the political sovereignty of Russia or its internal affairs. Their only objective should be to provide aid that would be acceptable to the Russian people "in their endeavor to regain control of their own affairs, their own territory, and their own destiny."[35]

Wilson obviously measured his decision to intervene against the principles of a future Russian policy which he had established half a year earlier in his Fourteen Points speech. In January he had announced that he would support a complete evacuation of all foreign troops from the Russian territory and the reconstruction of Russian territorial unity. In his memorandum of 17 July, he explained that his decision to support Allied military action in Russia was not a violation of his own principles. He announced that the Allies would only act in accordance with the wish of the majority of the Russian people. To Wilson, that statement implied the goal of overthrowing the Soviet government, since he believed that the Russian people were subjected to a dictatorial rule by the Bolsheviks. The refusal to grant diplomatic recognition to the Bolshevik government showed that he did not believe they acted in accordance with the desire of the Russian citizens.

There were many parallels between Wilson's protracted deci-
sion-making process to intervene in the First World War and his
intervention in Russia. In both cases, Wilson's initial reaction was
to remain aloof. Similarly, both decisions were preceded by Western European lobbying efforts and amounted to a gradual ration-
alization process by Wilson. In both instances, he finally did what
he at first had considered the wrong policy. As soon as he agreed
to cooperate with the Allies, however, he insisted that his decision
would serve overriding moral purposes, such as democracy and
self-determination.

But did Wilson believe a few thousand Allied troops were
necessary to protect the Czechoslovaks whose numbers were
believed to be between 50,000 and 70,000? An analysis of the
intervention itself sheds surprisingly little further light on the ideas
behind the dispatch of troops to Russia. In late summer 1918, the
United States sent 5,700 army draftees to the Arctic port city of
Archangel and 10,000 marines to Siberia. Such limited contingents
could not be considered a decisive factor in the Russian civil war.
Their areas of operation, moreover, lay in the northernmost parts
of Russia and in eastern Siberia, about 4,000 miles away from the
new capital, Moscow. In particular, the troops sent to Archangel
were unprepared for the extremely harsh conditions of Russian
Arctic winters and were poorly equipped. Their task of guarding
stores of military goods could not be accomplished because most
war matériel had been removed prior to the Americans' arrival. In
his study of the intervention in Archangel, historian Benjamin
Rhodes has observed that it was based on "misinformation, profound geographical and political misconceptions, and a generous
supply of wishful thinking." He called the intervention an "unusually inept" military campaign in historical comparison.[36] While
Archangel, Murmansk, and Vladivostok were central strategic
harbor cities for the Russian Empire, their importance as commercial harbors for the Soviet government in 1918 was diminished
because the country was excluded from foreign trade after the
revolution. Moreover, connections between those peripheral cities
and the center of Russia consisted of single train tracks. Despite
those limitations on the intervention, the fact remains that American troops were only a small part of an Allied Expeditionary Force,
consisting also of British and Japanese soldiers, which, with the

Czechoslovaks already in Siberia, actually provided aid to the many local anti-Soviet groups.

Wilson's decision to intervene in Russia received a mixed reaction. His close confidant Colonel House was far from elated when the president yielded to the advocates of intervention. He noted in his diary on 19 September 1918: "I disagree almost entirely with the manner in which the President has handled the Russian situation, although I agree heartily with the objects he has in view." House believed that it would have been more appropriate to provide economic aid to the Russians instead of presenting the United States as a primarily interventionist state.[37]

The liberal press also criticized Wilson's decision. Editorials in the *New Republic* at first welcomed the help for the Czechs but took an increasingly critical stand as the intervention continued and assumed a growing anti-Bolshevik focus. In contrast, *The Nation* stated that a military expedition to overthrow the Soviets would amount to declaring war against the Russian masses. Military intervention, it concluded, was the worst of all possible ways to relieve the Russian situation. Oswald Garrison Villard noted that the president had assured the American people that it was "only to be a little intervention, and we are to forgive it or approve it on the grounds of its littleness."[38]

Apart from the liberal and left criticism that the intervention interfered in the Russian civil war on the side of the antidemocratic forces, some contemporaries who took part in the intervention criticized Wilson for having failed to define the tasks the American troops were expected to fulfill in Russia. The order which Secretary of War Baker gave to the commanding general of the Expeditionary Army, William S. Graves, may serve as an example for this uncertainty. Graves himself publicly criticized the administration after the war for never having been told what his superiors expected him to do. The only basis for all military decisions Graves had to make in Siberia was Wilson's memorandum of 17 July, which Secretary Baker had handed him, saying: "This contains the policy of the United States in Russia which you are to follow."[39]

In a 1931 book, Graves presented his own interpretation of why the Allies desired intervention in 1918. In Graves's view, England and France were interested primarily in reestablishing the Eastern front: "French and English are, undoubtedly, trying to get the Allied forces committed to some act which will result in the establishment of an Eastern front." The second goal was to contain Bolshevism: "These [British and French] military representatives [in Vladivostok] not only did not deny, but boasted about their efforts to destroy, what they called, bolshevism." Graves made it clear that he did not share the British and French goals and considered them to stand in contrast to his orders.

Graves was far from sure whether Wilson had expected him to resist further anti-Bolshevik measures without stating that antirevolutionary aspect openly. The army's order was to defend Vladivostok against Bolshevik attacks to ensure the safe passage of Czechoslovak soldiers through the city. But when Graves arrived in the city, he noticed that the Czechs had already taken control of the Trans-Siberian Railway and most of the towns on the line and that they had decided not to leave the country. The Czechs obviously did not need American support. Did that imply that the official order did not reflect the Wilson administration's true political and military goals in the intervention? Graves believed that that was partially the case. He believed that the State and War departments followed different policies on Russia. Secretary of War Baker shared Graves's policy of maintaining equidistance from all Russian groups. Secretary Lansing, on the other hand, advocated supporting Russian anti-Bolshevik groups. Lansing had advised Ernest L. Harris, the American consul general in Irkutsk, a center for anti-Bolshevik resistance activity, "to keep in touch with the leaders of all movements and report regularly the progress of their endeavors, the development of the various efforts to establish law and order which are being made, and the strength and character of support from the Russian population which they attract."[40] Lansing continued that the United States was currently not prepared to grant official recognition to any of the anti-Soviet movements. The American administration's sympathy, however, was clearly on the side of the counterrevolutionary forces.

On 26 October 1918, Lansing drafted a memorandum on "Absolutism and Bolshevism" in which he called the Bolshevik ideology more dangerous than Prussian militarism. Bolshevism, he wrote, was "opposed to nationality and represents a great international movement of ignorant masses to overthrow governments everywhere. . . . Bolshevism is the most hideous and monstrous thing the human mind has ever conceived. . . . A Bolshevik Germany or Austria is too horrible to contemplate. It is worse, far worse, than a Prussianized Germany."[41] By the time Lansing wrote those lines, Allied troops had fought the Prussianized Germany for three years. Lansing noted on the eve of the victory in the First World War that an even more dangerous enemy had emerged. Should Allied troops remain in Russia after the German capitulation to fight that new danger? Lansing was not the only one to discuss that question. In a letter to Wilson on 27 November 1918, Secretary of War Baker expressed his doubts that a continuation of the intervention was morally justified after Germany's military capitulation. The reason that had led to the intervention four months earlier had disappeared. The Czech soldiers could safely be evacuated, and the stores of military supply did not have to be protected from German troops. Baker recommended an immediate removal of all U.S. troops from Russia. The Russians should solve their problems alone.[42]

In November 1918, Wilson also favored the complete removal of all foreign intervention troops. "My policy regarding Russia," he told Wiseman of the British intelligence office in the United States in October, "is very similar to my Mexican policy. I believe in letting them work out their own salvation, even though they wallow in anarchy for a while." But the president feared that removal of American soldiers would lead to Japanese domination over Siberia. On 27 November 1918, he wrote to Grenville Stanley Macfarland of the New York American: "My mind is not clear as to what is the immediate proper course in Russia. There are many more elements at work there than I can conjecture you are aware of, and it is harder to get out than it was to go in." In the fall of 1918, Wilson felt he had become a victim of his own concessions to the Allies. He had provided the intervention with moral legitimacy. Contrary to an agreement with the Allies, the government in Tokyo had sent a huge occupation army of between 60,000 and 70,000 soldiers to Siberia.[43] Siberia would have been left in the hands of the Japanese after a unilateral American withdrawal. An agreement leading to the evacuation of all foreign troops from Siberian soil was one of the goals of the peace conference that began in early 1919 in Paris.

The unspecific wording of the intervention order for Graves not only led to confusion among contemporaries, but also contributed to a controversial discussion in the American historiography about the goals of the intervention. While the president wanted the intervention to conform to the strictest moral standards, his *aide-*

memoire of 17 July, as historian Rhodes put it, "contributed to the 'sad confusion in Russia' he sought to clarify" by not providing the American troops with clear instructions about how far they were authorized to go in their support for the anti-Bolsheviks. In his study *The Decision to Intervene*, George F. Kennan doubted that there was any conclusive answer to the question of whether the Czech forces were consolidated to proceed to France or to participate in the Russian civil war. Liberals such as N. Gordon Levin believed that Wilson pursued two goals at the same time. The first one was directed against German imperialism, "yet it was equally true that anti-Bolshevism was both implicit and latent in the Siberian intervention." The Wilson administration, he believed, was never prepared to accept a Bolshevik rule in Russia to enlist the Red Army in the fight against Germany. Levin did not state explicitly whether Wilson considered the Bolsheviks to be a greater menace to the United States than the enemy in the war, Imperial Germany. Left-wing historians, such as William A. Williams, interpreted the intervention primarily under an anti-Bolshevik aspect: "The President saw the Czechs as a strong, effective force which he could support against the Bolsheviks, and one which was also anti-Japanese and anti-German. That was precisely the kind of nucleus he had been looking for since . . . April."[44]

It is beyond dispute that the intervention assumed an anti-Bolshevik character. But did Wilson plan it that way? Initially, the president rejected the idea of intervention on ideological grounds as well as because of its limited military value. Wilson was surprised by the persistent Allied requests to send troops to Siberia. During the spring and early summer of 1918, the president found himself in an increasingly isolated position. Between January and May 1918, the British and French ambassadors sent the U.S. government six formal requests for intervention. Wilson was opposed to the idea of Allied cooperation with the Bolsheviks and refused to recognize the Soviet government. An Allied agreement with the Bolsheviks on military and political issues would have dealt the democratic counterrevolution the final death blow. The anti-Soviet opposition could not have counted on further Allied aid and could not have resisted compromises with the Bolsheviks if Western democracies opened negotiations with them.[45]

But Wilson believed he could support the Czechoslovak troops without abandoning his ideological principles. The Czechs had no genuine interest in interfering in Russian affairs. Even after he had published his decision to intervene, he pointed out in a private conversation with Lord Reading that he considered any military action in Russia futile under the aspect of strengthening the Allied efforts in the war against Germany. The president, Reading reported to the Foreign Office, "was anxious that H.M.G[overnment]. should understand that it was really not possible for the U.S.G[overnment]. to embark on an enterprise of magnitude in Russia, for even though it should be carried out mainly by Japanese troops the equipment and supply would in the main have to come from the U.S. He . . . agreed with the opinion that it would be impossible for the U.S.G. to continue to supply and equip troops for the western front and also to undertake to provide for Japanese troops in Russia." Wilson could not have made it more obvious that he still disliked the idea of intervention and that he only agreed to it for reasons of Allied solidarity. The president told Secretary of War Baker, who disagreed with the president's decision to intervene, that he felt obliged to participate in the intervention "because the French and British were pressing it upon his attention so hard and he had refused so many of their requests that they were beginning to feel he was not a good associate, much less a good ally."[46]

Obviously, Wilson's decision to intervene has to be seen as the result of both an ideological confrontation with the Bolsheviks and the political necessity of Allied political and military coordination. In the negotiations leading up to the decision to intervene, Wilson tried to limit the scope of the military action. His original goal was to evacuate all foreign troops from a united democratic Russia. He considered the Bolshevik rule to be an obstacle to the democratization of the country. Therefore, he could agree to send U.S. troops as well. Wilson's promise not to interfere in Russia's internal affairs was fulfilled by not openly siding with any of the Russian civil war factions. The Allied Expeditionary Force's moral duty was to assist the struggle of the Russian people for democracy against the dominating autocratic clique. Therefore, Wilson's view of neutrality had an anti-Bolshevik tendency. Soviet rule had to be replaced by a democratically chosen government. But while his ideological convictions told him that Russian democracy would prevail without outside interference, his Allies urged him to accelerate the inevitable. "Almost miraculously, it seemed," historian Levin wrote, "events had conspired to present the Wilson administration with the opportunity in Siberia to support liberal Russian elements who were both anti-Bolshevik and anti-German." The Czechs made it possible for Wilson to reconcile his ideological opposition to intervention with the political need to support anti-revolutionary forces.[47] Wilson's justification for the intervention, however, depended on the continuation of the war in Europe. The armistice in November 1918 renewed the questions about the Allied intervention in Russia.

4

Intervention and the Paris Peace Conference: Wilson's Russian Policy in 1919

Were they [Western intervention troops] at war with Soviet Russia? Certainly not; but they shot Soviet Russians at sight. They stood as invaders on Russian soil. They armed the enemies of the Soviet government. . . . They earnestly desired and schemed its downfall. But war—shocking! Interference— shame! It was, they repeated, a matter of indifference to them how Russians settled their own internal affairs. They were impartial—Bang!
— Winston S. Churchill, *The Aftermath*, 1929[1]

On 11 November 1918, after more than four years of fighting, Germany signed an armistice agreement at Compiègne near Paris. With the fighting over, Allied politicians turned their attention to the next task, drafting a peace treaty. From January through June 1919, twenty-seven governments with more than 700 delegates met in Paris to decide on peace conditions for Germany and the other Central Powers, and to discuss the creation of a new postwar collective security organization, the League of Nations. The peace conference debated two aspects of the Russian problem. First, should Russian groups be admitted to the conference, and, if so, should the Bolsheviks or any other group be invited to represent Russia? Second, should the Allied occupation of Archangel and

Vladivostok be maintained after the initial justification of protecting stockpiles of matériel of strategic value from German troops, disappeared with the termination of the war?[2]

Against the advice of friends and members of his own cabinet, notably Secretary of State Lansing, President Wilson announced one week after the German capitulation that he would personally travel to Paris to chair the American delegation to the peace conference. Those who opposed Wilson's participation feared that he might become too closely identified with particular European war aims. The moment the president would sit down with his European counterparts at the conference, Frank Cobb of the New York *World* wrote to Colonel House in early November 1918, "he has lost all the power that comes from distance and detachment." Wilson would simply become "a negotiator dealing with other negotiators." Cobb's arguments did not impress the president. It was just because he was likely to be the only champion of a liberal and democratic peace that Wilson felt he had to attend the conference. When he read in a cable from Paris that both the French and British prime ministers Georges Clemenceau and David Lloyd George had expressed their hope that the president would not join the conference,[3] he reacted angrily. "I infer," he wrote to House, "that the French and English leaders desire to exclude me from the Conference for fear I might there lead the weaker nations against them."[4]

After the end of the war, Wilson returned to the earlier dichotomy of U.S. versus European political goals. Between August 1914 and April 1917, he had maintained that the aims of all European states in the war were similarly designed to further narrow nationalistic interests. Instead of supporting either side, Wilson endorsed a strict American neutrality. Only after he became convinced in the spring of 1917 that a German victory could lead to political and military threats and to economic difficulties for the United States did he change his rhetoric to justify an American entry into the war to fight for democracy. After November 1918, he again considered himself the only true champion of democracy, and he insisted that his presence was necessary at the Paris Peace Conference for establishing a liberal-democratic peace.

Wilson was correct in his assessment of the postwar goals of the Allies. The British delegation, headed by Lloyd George, and the

French negotiators, under Clemenceau, took positions different from Wilson's. England and France had suffered heavily during the war, far more heavily than the United States. And while huge crowds cheered Wilson during his visits to Paris and London before the conference, the French and British people also demanded revenge and restitution for the destruction of the war.

Lloyd George and Clemenceau were under considerable domestic pressure to seek German payments for the suffering and destruction of the long and bloody war. The members of the British and French delegations resented Wilson's constant high-minded appeals to higher principles. In their diaries, letters, and memoirs, they revealed their apprehension about Wilson's "sermonettes" on idealistic goals for which Europeans had fought for years while the United States remained on the sidelines. Despite the warnings from friends like House and Cobb, Wilson appeared unaware of the level of disagreement and personal resentment between his views and those of the Europeans.[5]

The peace conference convened at the Quai d'Orsay, the seat of the French foreign ministry, on 12 January 1919. One of the first issues on the agenda of the conference was to determine whether Russian representatives should be admitted to the negotiations. Prime Minister Lloyd George criticized the Allies for having failed to agree on a joint Russian policy. They had troops in Russia that were not sufficient in size to affect the civil war there. Those troops had to be reinforced or withdrawn. Lloyd George suggested that the Soviets as the de facto Russian government should participate in the peace conference. The Western states had recognized the tsarist government, "although at the time we knew it to be absolutely rotten." It was possible, he continued, that the "Bolshevists did not represent Russia. But certainly Prince Lvoff did not."[6]

Lloyd George's reasoning was pragmatic. Peace was unattainable, he later wrote in his *Memoirs of the Peace Conference*, as long as the largest country in Europe was left outside of the covenant of nations. Despite the West's hope for a quick end to Bolshevism, it appeared to be the most favored political group among the Russian workers and peasants. If the Western states considered Bolshevism to be as dangerous to world civilization as German militarism, he asked, who was going to carry out the attacks on Russia? He told the Paris Peace Conference that to "set Russia in order by force was a task which he for one would not invite Britain to undertake." If the peace conference would not agree to invite the Soviets to Paris, the conference should try to get all interested Russian groups together at a neutral place. That was the origin of the Principo proposal of late January that will be described later in this chapter.[7]

The French government, however, maintained a strictly anti-Bolshevik policy and rejected Lloyd George's suggestion of Soviet participation at the conference. Clemenceau declared that he was opposed to conversations with the Bolsheviks because "we would be raising them to our level by saying that they were worthy of entering into conversations with us." Clemenceau's anti-Bolshevik attitude was based on a number of considerations. France had felt much greater effects when Russia left the war in 1918 than any other country, including Great Britain. After the treaty of Brest-Litovsk, Germany used the opportunity to increase its forces fighting on French soil. France also had the most to lose if the Bolsheviks stayed in power. French banks had invested large sums of money in Russia since the turn of the century. They feared for those investments if the Bolsheviks stayed in power. Finally, Clemenceau was afraid that the Soviet delegation might use its stay in Paris for propaganda purposes, especially to make revolutionary calls to the French workers.[8]

President Wilson had considered the question of Russian representation at the conference soon after the signing of the armistice agreement. On 20 November, he received a memorandum from Boris Bakhmet'ev, the ambassador of the former Russian Provisional Government in Washington, in which the envoy urged the United States to invite Russia to the upcoming peace conference. He reminded the president of his country's contribution to the war from August 1914 through December 1917 and pleaded that the Russian people, "unhappy enough to be the first victim of the social disease now threatening the world," should not be excluded from the peace negotiations. Wilson immediately asked Lansing whether it was feasible to have one representative of Russia at the conference despite the disintegration of the country into various parts. In his reply, Lansing insisted that only delegates from governments based on democratic principles should be invited to become signatories to the peace treaty. In the interim, however, representatives "from existing elements of order," meaning anti-Bolshevik groups, could be invited to take part in the conference proceedings.[9]

Wilson disagreed with Lansing's view that a number of anti-Bolshevik groups should be officially invited to the conference. While Lansing apparently did not reject the breakup of Russia into a number of independent states as the result of the peace conference, Wilson's thinking centered around maintaining Russia as an undivided country. Inviting various groups could be a first step toward dividing Russia by recognizing a multitude of individual governments. Wilson, therefore, preferred not to grant recognition to any of the various self-proclaimed governments.[10]

In this situation, the Soviets sent a long letter to Wilson which the president received on Christmas Eve 1918, when he was already in Europe for the peace conference. In the letter, Maxim M. Litvinov, the assistant Soviet commissar for foreign affairs, urged Wilson to end the intervention in Russia, to grant the Soviet government diplomatic recognition, and to help Russians launch their economic recovery. Two political courses were open to the peace conference, Litvinov wrote. One was intervention and prolongation of the war, and the "further embitterment of the Russian masses," the devastation of the country, and terror by the anti-Bolshevik White Russian groups. The alternative was to "help Russia to regain her own sources of supply, and to give her technical advice how to exploit her natural richness . . . for the benefit of all countries badly in need of foodstuffs and raw materials."[11]

Litvinov's letter was devoid of insults and accusations and appealed to Wilson's liberalism and to his "sense of justice and impartiality." It concluded with a plea for Soviet participation in the Paris conference: "I hope and trust, above all, that before deciding on any course of action you will give justice to the demand of *audiatur et altera pars* [let the other side be heard, too]." Wilson considered the Soviet demand justified and shared his thoughts on the subject with British Prime Minister David Lloyd George. Litvinov's letter might have been one of the reasons for Wilson's repeated calls for Soviet participation in an informal gathering of all Russian civil war factions, even though he had decided in advance not to grant them recognition as the legitimate Russian government.[12]

On the same occasion of his visit to the British capital, Wilson could have met with his ambassador to Russia, David Francis, who was scheduled to undergo surgery at a London hospital in early January. The president, however, missed the opportunity to get further advice on the Russian problem and did not meet with Francis before the opening of the Peace Conference. While Wilson's schedule undoubtedly was tight in the days prior to the Paris meeting, it also seems clear that he was in no rush to receive Francis's information about Russia and recommendations for a future policy toward the Bolsheviks. A meeting between the two men finally took place aboard the U.S.S. *George Washington* in February 1919 during Wilson's midconference journey back to the United States. In that meeting, Francis took a hard-line position on the Bolsheviks and recommended sending 50,000 American soldiers to Russia to protect him when he would return to Petrograd as ambassador without recognizing the Bolshevik government. Wilson thought it was impossible to maintain troops in Europe after the signing of a peace treaty and considered it unlikely that 50,000 men would volunteer for that assignment.[13]

American preconference documents reveal the extent of Wilson's deliberations with members of the American commission about the problem of Russia and Bolshevism. General Tasker H. Bliss recorded a meeting with the president and other members of the American delegation on 7 January in his diary. In the meeting, Bliss made it clear that he considered it futile to attempt to contain Bolshevism with military means. An army could prevent Bolsheviks from crossing a demarcation line but could not prevent *Bolshevism* from doing so. The gravest danger that Bliss foresaw was the spread of Bolshevism into Germany. He recommended building up a strong democratic government in Germany "which will be the natural barrier between Western Europe and Russian Bolshevism." The president and other members of the commission, Bliss noted, agreed.[14]

Wilson's Russian policy in early 1919 developed by eliminating the three options that he objected to most vigorously. First, he rejected the recognition of Soviet domination of Russia as a violation of democratic liberalism and refused to consider them the official Russian representative at the Paris Peace Conference. But second, he also rejected plans to overthrow the Bolsheviks by outside force and acknowledged that the Soviet regime was the dominant political force in Russia at the moment. Third, Wilson refused to consider a breakup of Russia into a number of independent states. His solution to this quandary was that no Russian group should be represented *officially* at the conference. *Unofficial* groups, however, should be welcome to argue their positions in Paris.[15]

The question of Russian representation played a dominant role during the first weeks of the conference. On 20 January 1919, Joseph Noulens, the French ambassador to Russia, reported conditions in Soviet Russia to the Council of Ten. The image he painted was one of exploitation, terror, and despair there. Despite exerting considerable pressure on the electorate, the Soviets had lost the constitutional election in December 1917. Instead of accepting the defeat and relinquishing power, they broke up the Assembly shortly after it had constituted itself. In January 1918, Noulens continued, Trotsky had threatened that if the Soviet government faced resistance, it would enforce its power "by a terror unexampled in history." The day after Noulens's report to the conference, the Danish ambassador to Russia, Eric de Scavenius, painted a similar picture of Bolshevik horrors. He emphasized the threat that Germany might follow Russia's example of a Bolshevik revolution. Political unrest in Germany was so far following the course of the Russian Revolution, he said. It was currently at the stage that Russia had reached in July 1917.[16]

After de Scavenius's presentation to the peace conference, Wilson read a report by William H. Buckler about his talks with the Russian representative, Maxim M. Litvinov. The president had sent Buckler, a member of the United States embassy in London, to Stockholm for talks with a Soviet representative. In his conversations with Buckler in mid-January, Litvinov announced wide-ranging political concessions if the Allies would immediately terminate the intervention and would grant diplomatic recognition to the Council of Peoples' Commissars as government. He promised "to compromise on all points, including the Russian foreign debt, protecting of existing foreign enterprises and the granting of new concessions in Russia." The Soviets would stop all revolutionary propaganda abroad and would release political prisoners.[17]

Litvinov's offer was still vague, however. He did not specify to what extent the Soviets would accept liability for prerevolutionary Russian private and public debts. Nevertheless, his willingness to offer negotiations about the debt issue was an indication that the Soviets were very interested in achieving better relations with the Allies. Litvinov indicated a Soviet willingness to cooperate and compromise with the Western democracies and even admitted mistakes the Soviet government had made in its treatment of the "intelligentsia" and the peasants immediately after the revolution.[18]

The reasons for the Soviet policy of seeking cooperation with the Allies were apparent. The hope of a socialist world revolution had not materialized. Russia remained the only socialist country in the world; its government faced the challenges of a civil war and the continued occupation of two important harbors, Archangel and Vladivostok, by foreign troops. In that difficult situation, the Soviet regime had few alternatives to pursuing a traditional foreign policy of seeking better relations with its neighbors.

Despite the apparent vagueness, Wilson welcomed Litvinov's offer. William C. Bullitt, a State Department official and member of the American delegation at Paris, testified in September 1919 that the president had been impressed by the concessions the Soviets offered. French Prime Minister Clemenceau, however, remained unconvinced by the Soviet concessions when Wilson announced them on 21 January. The French continued to refuse granting the Bolsheviks entry visas into France. Clemenceau told his colleagues that he could imagine the Soviet propaganda reaction to acceptance of the Bolsheviks after they promised to uphold property rights: "We [Soviets] offered them great principles of justice, and the Allies would have nothing to do with us. Now we offer money, and they are ready to make peace."[19]

The views that various experts like Noulens and Buckler presented at the conference demonstrated the gap between those groups that advocated improved relations with the Soviets and those that abhorred their rule and advocated their violent overthrow. As a compromise between the more conciliatory American and British position on the one hand, and the hard-line French views on the other, Wilson took up an earlier British proposal and suggested a meeting between the Russian civil war parties and the Allies at a neutral place. He urged the Western European statesmen to demonstrate their willingness to negotiate with all Russian factions. His arguments for including the Soviets in the negotiations showed his interest in providing a liberal position in response to the Soviet pleas to have a voice in all decisions concerning Russia. Wilson stressed that by opposing Bolshevism with force, the Allies had made it possible for the Soviets to argue that "Imperialistic and Capitalistic Governments were endeavoring to exploit the country and to give the land back to the landlords, and so bring about a reaction. If it could be shown that this was not true and that the Allies were prepared to deal with the rulers of Russia, much of the moral forces of this argument would disappear."[20]

Wilson's suggestion for a conference of all Russian civil war parties was another example of his amalgamation of ideological rhetoric with pragmatic goals. He insisted that the Bolsheviks should be participants at a conference that would determine the future of Russia. He even sent envoys to Moscow to talk to the Soviet leadership directly about their political goals. At the same time, however, there were few indications that he would have ever agreed to grant the Soviets diplomatic recognition. His political goals were as anti-Bolshevik as those of Clemenceau; he still believed that a liberal-democratic political system was far superior to the Bolshevik one. He only differed with the French premier in the way to achieve democracy in Russia. Wilson believed that if the Allies would modify their policy and would start negotiating with all Russian political groups, this would lead to diminishing support for the Bolsheviks among the Russian people. If the Allies could "swallow their pride and the natural repulsion which they felt for the Bolsheviks, and see the representatives of all organized groups in one place, he thought it would bring about a marked reaction against Bolshevism."[21]

In contrast to his European colleagues, however, Wilson did not believe he could pursue this policy without a liberal invitation to all Russian civil war factions. Wilson was convinced in early 1919 that the Russians would turn away from Bolshevism if the anti-Soviet groups would present themselves as aspiring to create a democratic state. Wilson did not see a contradiction between his liberal Russian policy—inviting the Bolsheviks to a conference on Russia—and his opposition to Bolshevism because free people would always choose a democratic government over a dictatorship.

Wilson's political vision for Russia depended on two preconditions that came out of the American political tradition and whose validity in the Russian situation he never seriously questioned. First, he equated anti-Bolshevism with democracy. Second, his theory implied that the anti-Soviet movements in Russia shared his optimism that the Bolsheviks could be defeated without foreign support. As it turned out, neither of those preconditions applied. Wilson himself had written in one of his early essays on politics that democracy was "wrongly conceived when treated merely as a body of doctrine." Instead, it was a "stage of development." "Immature people," he wrote, "cannot have it."[22] In his Russian policy he did exactly what he had once criticized. He treated democracy merely as a set of rules of policy to be applied in the Russian situation under the most adverse circumstances. Battle-scarred Russia with its thousand-year-long tradition of autocracy was a particularly poor candidate for introducing democracy in 1919. Second, in contrast to Wilson's hopes, anti-Bolshevik groups believed they needed foreign help to topple the Soviets. Therefore, during the peace conference, former tsarist military officers repeatedly sought Wilson's support in their fight against Bolshevism.

On 21 January, the European Allies agreed with Wilson's suggestion that a conference of all Russian civil war parties be held in a neutral country. Wilson himself drafted a resolution inviting every organized group that was exercising "political authority or military control anywhere in Siberia, or within the boundaries of European Russia," to send representatives to a conference on the Principo Island in the Sea of Marmora.[23] Each party should be represented by three delegates. The Soviet delegates who represented the de facto government of European Russia would face nine anti-Soviet delegates, representing the regional governments of Archangel, Omsk, and Samara. By admitting numerous Russian groups to a conference, the associated powers officially assumed a neutral stance toward all Russian civil war factions and took a middle position between refusing to deal with the Bolsheviks and de facto recognition.

The official invitation to the conference, drafted by Wilson, contained the statement that the associated powers

recognize the revolution without reservation, and will in no way, and in no circumstances, aid or give countenance to any attempt at counter-revolution. It is not their wish or purpose to favour or assist any one of those organized groups now contending for the leadership and guidance of Russia as against the others.[24]

Almost everything in those two sentences requires an interpretation. Which revolution did the Allies recognize "without reservation?" Most historians believe that Wilson referred to the February Revolution and not the Bolshevik coup d'état of October. But if the Allies pledged not to aid the counterrevolution, how could they also invite the Bolsheviks, the greatest threat to Russian democracy, to a conference with the other Russian parties? And how could Wilson claim in June 1919, more than a year after the Allies had imposed a complete economic blockade on Soviet Russia and half a year after the beginning of the military intervention, that they would not favor any of the groups in Russia? Historians have suggested various ways to solve that contradiction. N. Gordon Levin noted that the statement indicated Wilson's unbiased position to view the Bolsheviks either as a "criminal force to be excluded from the political process, or as one Russian political faction among many to be absorbed into a pluralistic and competitive liberal order." The president, however, was not prepared to accept a situation in which the "Bolsheviks would abolish liberalism and maintain single-party rule." In other words, Wilson would deal with the Bolsheviks only if they became a conservative political force. Other historians have interpreted Wilson's statement in more critical terms. John M. Thompson noted that the text of the invitation to Principo reflected Wilson's "inability at times to distinguish between what was and what ought to be." In fact, the statement indicated the perfect Western policy on the Russian crisis: recognition of the democratic revolution and a pledge to be impartial in the current civil war. That was what Wilson, the ideologue, considered the best policy. In terms of *realpolitik*, however, it was not a viable option because the Bolsheviks were the dominant group and the Allied states did not want to see a socialist victory in Russia.[25]

Even though it was forced into a minority role at the meeting, the Soviet government on 4 February 1919 declared its willingness to participate in the conference. The Soviets also offered concessions in four different areas. They agreed to recognize Russia's foreign debts, to grant mining concessions to foreigners, to discuss territorial problems, and to refrain from interfering in Allied internal affairs. Those were important concessions for the Soviets. Historians have even compared the Soviet response to the Principo proposal with the acceptance of the harsh Brest-Litovsk Treaty. Again, Lenin accepted humiliation to ensure the survival of the regime, despite considerable resistance to such concessions within the Bolshevik party.[26]

The question of whether the Soviets were indeed willing to offer such wide-ranging compromises or whether they were playing for time will probably never be answered satisfactorily because the peace conference gave up the proposal within two weeks. All other civil war parties refused to cooperate with the Bolsheviks. In a joint note to the Paris Peace Conference, the "unified governments of Siberia, Archangel and Southern Russia" maintained that "under no circumstances whatever, would there be any question of an exchange of ideas on this matter with the participation of the Bolshevists, in whom the conscience of the Russian people sees only traitors."[27] The Russian resistance groups did not consider the conference an opportunity to present themselves to the Western statesmen and to the world. They were afraid that as the outcome of the meeting the Soviets would be considered the de facto government of Russia. Unlike Wilson, the resistance groups were not convinced that the Bolsheviks could be overthrown exclusively from within Russia. Moreover, they believed that a compromise between the civil war factions was inconceivable. If the Allies had decided to evacuate Russia as the result of the Principo conference, the Bolsheviks would have easily secured their dominant position. The resistance groups' goal was to keep the Allies involved in Russian affairs and to prevent them from negotiating with the Bolsheviks.

On 14 February, the Allies deliberated about their own reaction to the anti-Soviet groups' refusal to participate in the conference. Wilson admitted that he was uncertain about many issues concerning Russia but that he had a clear opinion about two points. He advocated the evacuation of all Allied troops: "Allied and Associate Powers were doing no sort of good in Russia. They did not know for whom or for what they were fighting. They were not assisting any promising common effort to establish order throughout Russia." The second point related to Principo. What the Allies sought "was not a *rapprochement* with the Bolsheviks, but clear information." This goal still had to be pursued. As far as he was concerned, he would be quite content that informal American representatives should meet representatives from the Bolsheviks.[28]

In mid-February, the Allies' Russian policy reached an impasse. On 8 February, Lloyd George had left for London, and Wilson was scheduled to return to Washington for a few weeks after the closing of the meeting on 14 February. On the day of Wilson's departure from Paris, the British minister for war production, Winston Churchill, who, as Lloyd George put it in his memoirs, "adroitly seized the opportunity" of the prime minister's absence, tried to influence

the conference in an anti-Bolshevik direction. He urged the delegations to take joint military action to enable the Russian armies to
continue fighting the Bolsheviks. In his reply to Churchill's proposal, Wilson repeated that the Allied troops were doing no good
in Russia and rejected Churchill's proposal. The president erred,
however, if he believed that his objections would end consideration
of Churchill's proposal. After Wilson's departure on 15 February,
the Council again took up that issue. General Alby, the French chief
of staff, presented a report in which he pointed out that the
Bolsheviks had turned Allied indecision to their advantage. Regular
Allied troops, he maintained, could easily defeat the Red Army.[29]

Wilson expressed his surprise and dismay when he learned on
19 February, while still on board the U.S.S. *George Washington* en
route to Boston, that the conference had further discussed anti-Bolshevik measures in his absence. In a cable to Paris he warned the
American Commission to Negotiate Peace that it would be "fatal to
be led further into the Russian chaos."[30]

The same day that Wilson warned about further involvement in
Russia, Clemenceau fell victim to an assassination attempt. Lloyd
George told House after that incident that "as long as Clemenceau
was wounded and was ill, he was the boss of the roost, and that
anything he desired to veto would be immediately wiped out and
therefore it was no use for him and Colonel House . . . to attempt
to renew the Principo proposal."[31]

In this impasse in the joint Western policy toward Russia, House
decided to send an envoy to Russia. As emissary he chose William
C. Bullitt, a twenty-eight-year-old former reporter for the *Philadelphia Public Ledger* who had only joined the State Department in
December 1917. Bullitt's liberal views and his opposition to the
military intervention in Russia were well known at the time. In
February 1918, Bullitt had sent House a memorandum in which he
noted that "[e]very principle of liberalism impels toward the recognition of the Soviet." He added that Soviet Commissar Trotsky was
"the sort of man we need to have in power in Russia and I think
that we should do everything possible to strengthen his hands. . . .
Trotsky is a good deal ahead of us in the march toward world
liberalism, but he is marching in our direction, and we must
support him or Nihilism will follow." On his journey to Russia,
Bullitt was accompanied by Lincoln Steffens, a "muckraking"

journalist who in 1918 had written an introduction to Leon Trotsky's book *The Bolsheviki and the World Peace*.[32]

In their pro-Soviet views, Bullitt and Steffens reflected neither the views of President Wilson, nor those of the other American peace negotiators. As with Wilson's selection of Elihu Root to travel to Russia almost two years earlier, it is not easy to understand why House chose Bullitt and Steffens for their mission. In both cases, it was the administration's obvious intention to choose envoys it considered to be friendly to the regime with which they were dealing. But while sending such an envoy ensured a friendly reception in Russia, it also had obvious disadvantages. Conservative politicians in the United States and at the Paris Peace Conference who rejected entering into contacts with the Bolsheviks could charge that Bullitt and Steffens were not critical enough toward their Russian counterparts. British Prime Minister Lloyd George told Bullitt after his return from Moscow that somebody who was known to be a "complete conservative" should have been sent instead of him.[33]

Bullitt himself called his mission an attempt to "obtain from the Soviet government an exact statement of the terms on which they were ready to stop fighting." In a 1919 Senate hearing into the Wilson administration's Russian policy, he claimed that House had authorized him to discuss issues with the Soviet leadership as crucial as the complete Allied withdrawal from Russia. Bullitt recalled a conversation in which House announced far-reaching Western concessions to the Soviets. When he asked:

[I]f the Bolsheviks are ready to stop the forward movement of their troops on all fronts . . . would we be willing to do likewise? . . . . [I]s the United States Government . . . prepared to press the Allies for a joint statement that all Allied troops will be withdrawn from . . . Russia as soon as practicable? Col. House replied that we were prepared to.[34]

Prior to his departure for Russia, Bullitt also discussed the goals of his mission with Philip Kerr, the private secretary to Lloyd George. Kerr told him that Great Britain would like to evacuate its troops from Archangel, and assured him that the prime minister would agree to end the intervention if the Soviets would guarantee the existence of all de facto governments on Russian soil.[35]

Bullitt left Paris on 22 February and arrived in Petrograd on 8 March 1919. He first conferred with Georgi V. Chicherin, Trotsky's successor as people's commissar for foreign affairs, and with Maxim Litvinov. Both assured him that the Soviet government wanted to end the hostilities and participate in a peace conference.[36] On 10 March, Bullitt traveled to Moscow, where on 14 March Lenin handed him an official Soviet peace proposal. According to the Soviet offer, all parties should immediately start armistice negotiations on the basis that "all existing *de facto* governments which have been set up on the territory of the former Russian Empire and Finland [are] to remain in full control of the territories which they occupy at the moment when the armistice becomes effective." The Soviet government agreed to accept the counterrevolutionary rule in certain parts of Russia if those groups would stop fighting the Bolshevik rule in areas where they dominated. Lenin also announced a general amnesty as soon as the civil war was over. He sought the following promises from the Allies:

Immediately after the signing of this agreement, all troops of the Allied and Associated Governments and other non-Russian governments to be withdrawn from Russia and military assistance to cease to be given to anti-Soviet Governments which have been set up on the territory of the former Russian Empire.[37]

On 16 March, Bullitt cabled the American delegation at the Paris Peace Conference that there was "no doubt whatever of the desire of the Soviet Government for a just and reasonable peace, or of the sincerity of the proposal." Bullitt got the impression that the Soviet government was firmly established in Petrograd and Moscow. Former opposition parties, particularly the Mensheviks, now supported Lenin "because Russia was being attacked from outside and threatened by more drastic intervention." Living conditions in Russia were harsh, Bullitt continued, mainly because of the Allied blockade. But Bullitt also saw the potential for a violent overthrow of the Bolshevik rule. The Allies "can overthrow the Communists if we are considering to continue the economic blockade and intervention indefinitely, we can produce . . . famine, hunger and battles for bread." Bullitt warned against such a policy: "Then we shall finally have to intervene over the dead bodies and dead hopes of the simple Russian people." He suggested that the Allies should consider Lenin's proposal and should be willing to compromise with the Bolsheviks.[38]

In his talks with Bullitt, Lenin continued the Soviet policy of accepting painful cuts into the state's territorial integrity that had earlier guided the decisions at Brest-Litovsk and in response to the Principo proposal. Lenin proposed a dismemberment of Russia into a number of independent states, some of them governed by anti-Bolshevik groups. Lenin's ultimate goal was the evacuation of all foreign troops from Russia. After all Western armies had left Russian territory, the Soviets believed that sooner or later they would be successful in the civil war.[39]

Prior to Lenin's proposal, the Western Allies had discussed Russian affairs in terms of a socialism versus democracy dichotomy. The Soviet concessions following the Principo invitation and Lenin's proposal to Bullitt forced them to rethink the premises of their Russian policy. In particular, the question now was whether the Allies could accept a socialist Russia that would conduct a "regular capitalist" foreign economic policy. The lack of a clearly defined position on that question became obvious when Bullitt sent copies of Lenin's peace proposal, along with his own recommendations to accept them, to Wilson, Lloyd George, and House.[40]

After his return from Russia on 25 March, Bullitt briefed the American and British delegations extensively about the situation in Russia. The American Commission disagreed about a response to Lenin's proposal, with Lansing rejecting it and House willing to explore it further. Prime Minister Lloyd George invited Bullitt to a private meeting to discuss Russian affairs on 26 March. In that meeting, the prime minister told him that Great Britain was momentarily not in a position to change its Russian policy. Public opinion would not tolerate such a step. Bullitt later testified before a Senate Committee about his trip to Russia and the Allies' reaction to Lenin's proposal: "Mr. Lloyd George said that he did not know what he could do with British public opinion. He had a copy of the *Daily Mail* in his hand, and he said, 'As long as the British press is doing this kind of thing how can you expect me to be sensible about Russia?' " The *Daily Mail*, Bullitt complained, "was roaring and screaming about the whole Russian situation."[41]

Both Wilson and Lloyd George decided not to enter into any further official negotiations with the Bolsheviks. But unlike the British prime minister, Wilson never gave a reason for his decision. Bullitt got the impression that the president was unwilling to discuss Russian matters at all. House told him that he "had seen the President and the President had said he [Wilson] had a one-track mind and was occupied with Germany at present, and that he could not think about Russia."[42]

Bullitt did not believe that Wilson had lost interest in Russian affairs. Instead, he blamed Wilson's disinterest in Lenin's proposal on the sudden success of the "White" Admiral Aleksandr V. Kolchak in Siberia in March and April. The president, as Bullitt put it, expected a collapse of the Soviet government and was therefore not interested in an agreement with them:

Just at the moment, when this proposal was under consideration, Kolchak made a 100–mile advance . . . immediately the entire press of Paris was roaring and screaming on the subject, announcing that Kolchak would be in Moscow within two weeks; and therefore everyone in Paris, including, I regret to say, members of the American commission, began to grow very lukewarm about peace in Russia, because they thought Kolchak would . . . wipe out the Soviet Government.[43]

Bullitt observed a growing anti-Bolshevik sentiment among U.S. delegates to the peace conference. But it seems doubtful whether Kolchak's advance was the only reason for this anti-Soviet attitude. In the months of March and April, there were three further reasons not to conclude a peace agreement with the Bolsheviks.

First, Bullitt himself pointed out the anti-Bolshevik mood of the press and public opinion in Western Europe and the United States. The fear of a spread of revolution was intensified by strikes that paralyzed public life in Great Britain, by Bela Kun's Bolshevik coup d'état in Hungary on 23 March 1919, and by Lenin's proclamation of a Communist International. Those events met with sharp criticism in Europe and made it virtually impossible for democratically elected politicians to enter into negotiations with the Soviets.

The second factor was Wilson's health. On 4 April, the president suffered a breakdown, which medical historian Edwin Weinstein has diagnosed as a severe cold accompanied by high fever that caused heart and brain damage.[44] While Wilson was only recovering slowly from his collapse, Lenin's deadline for acceptance of his proposal expired on 10 April. Wilson had not been physically able to check the Soviet suggestions carefully.

Third, in early April the polar explorer Fridjof Nansen suggested ways to offer the Russian population humanitarian help. In a letter drafted by Herbert Hoover, the director general of relief of the

Supreme Economic Council, Nansen suggested organizing a "purely humanitarian Commission" for the provisoning of Russia. He wrote that it did "not appear that the existing authorities in Russia would refuse the intervention of such a Commission of wholly non-political order."[45] The letter asked the Allies for help in purchasing and distributing relief aid in Russia.

The Council of Four in Paris debated this proposal in early April. The goal of the Allies was to present a positive reply to Nansen simultaneously as a reaction to Lenin's peace proposal. On 17 April, the Allies assured Nansen of their support: "It seems to us that such a Commission as you propose would offer a practical means of achieving the beneficent results you have in view, and could not . . . be considered as having any other aim than the humanitarian purpose of saving life."[46] The transportation and distribution of the aid was difficult to manage in a country torn by civil war. The Allies suggested that the inhabitants of each Russian village should advise a relief organization that had to be founded for this purpose "upon the methods and personnel by which their community is to be relieved." The relief supply was to be transported to every village by neutral relief workers, "under no other condition could it be certain that the hungry would be fed." To facilitate this humanitarian action, the Allies called for the immediate termination of the civil war in Russia.

The various civil war parties in Russia, had mixed reactions to the Nansen plan. Soviet Commissar Chicherin wrote to Nansen that the Russians were indeed suffering. The cause, however, was the "inhuman blockade" of Russia by the Allied and associated states. Russia did not need aid: "If left in peace and allowed free development Soviet Russia would soon be able to restore her national production, to regain her economic strength, to provide for her own needs and to be helpful to other countries." Despite his criticism, Chicherin also announced that the Soviets would participate in the program.[47]

Admiral Kolchak, the head of the most important anti-Bolshevik countergovernment, the All-Russian Provisional Government in Omsk, Siberia, rejected Nansen's offer. In his view, only the Soviets would profit from the outside aid. His government already received Allied support, and one of his military tactics was to stir up unrest within Soviet-dominated areas by making food deliveries difficult. According to Nansen's plan, aid would be delivered to all war parties, including the Bolsheviks. On 4 May, the Russian Political Conference, whose members included former Prime Minsiter L'vov, rejected the proposal.[48]

Again, only the Bolsheviks had accepted an Allied proposal. On 16 May the Allies urged Nansen not to enter into negotiations with the Soviets.[49] After the failure of the Principo proposal, the Bullitt mission, and the Nansen offer, it became obvious that a compromise solution between the Russian parties was impossible to reach. The anti-Bolshevik groups resisted all proposals that would have forced them to negotiate with the Soviets and that would lead to an evacuation of the Allied armies. A termination of the intervention, as became increasingly clear in 1919, would have led to the Bolsheviks' immediate success in the civil war. This victory would to a large extent have been the result of the counterrevolutionaries' inability to find support for their fight among the population.

The best example of this inability is provided by Alexander Kolchak. Aided by the British army, he had become head of the Omsk-based All-Russian Provisional Government in mid-November 1918 and claimed the title of Supreme Ruler of all Russia. As a former tsarist officer, he was believed to be trying to reinstate the old tsarist monarchy. After military successes in the Volga region in April and May 1919, Kolchak's armies steadily lost ground because of the minimal support he received from the population and the disunity among the leaders of the various counterrevolutionary movements. In November 1919, the Red Army captured Omsk. Kolchak escaped to Irkutsk where he was soon captured and shot by the Bolsheviks. Historian Patrick A. Taylor characterized Kolchak's officers as virulent anti-Semites whose senseless shooting of thousands of possible allies ruined Siberia as a base of White operations. Kolchak's British-trained army came to number about 100,000 men, Taylor estimates, "but its morale was never high."[50]

Kolchak's temporary military success in the spring of 1919 led to tensions between him and General Graves, the commander of the American troops in Russia. Graves tried to maintain an equal distance from all civil war factions and steadfastly refused to acknowledge territorial claims by any of the various armies. It was the prerogative of the administration in Washington, he insisted, to recognize Russian governments.

Graves's conflict with Kolchak began in the spring of 1919 when the Russian officer claimed to be in charge of eastern Siberia. In early May, Graves asked the War Department in Washington to define U.S. policy in Siberia in light of Kolchak's recent military successes. The Western European Allies, Graves pointed out, considered the U.S. army in Siberia to be a "source of weakness to Kolchak."[51] "The fact that we are the only foreign power not here supporting Kolchak causes Russians who believe in American form of government to mistrust and oppose him." Graves even saw danger in a continuation of the old policy that might lead to the outbreak of violent conflicts with Kolchak. He only saw two possible solutions to this problem: "Using force or getting out." The policy of neutrality had to be defended or given up.

Wilson's halfhearted participation in the intervention posed a dilemma for Graves. The president refused to increase the number of soldiers, which would have been necessary to maintain the former policy of neutrality. Wilson feared that Japan then would also send additional troops to Siberia. That would pose the danger that the entire Russian Far East would fall under Tokyo's influence. For the same reason, Wilson opposed the immediate withdrawal of all U.S. troops. In the meantime, Graves had to prevent a military confrontation with Kolchak with insufficient troops at his disposal.[52]

In this situation, Wilson suggested to the Council of Four a plan to "democratize" the anti-Bolshevik resistance groups. He knew that Kolchak's success depended on Allied aid: "If supplies were stopped, Kolchak and Denikin would have to stop fighting too." Wilson submitted a proposal he had received from Alexander Kerensky. It stated that the Allies "should only help the various Russian groups on certain fundamental conditions for the establishing of Russia on a democratic basis with a constituent assembly, and Governments which declined to agree should not be supported." The final clause stated that "proposals for supplying food were harmful."[53]

The Allies agreed that an increase in the number of Western troops in Russia was as undesirable as a Bolshevik victory in the civil war. After they had failed to get White support for meetings with the Bolsheviks, they took a last effort and decided to aid the anti-Bolshevik forces in Russia. Wilson's suggestion contained a number of decidedly anti-Soviet clauses. References to the Constituent Assembly that Lenin had dissolved in January 1918 implied that Wilson had given up on the idea of Soviet participation in establishing a democratic government. When Lloyd George interjected that the proposal would split up Russia, Wilson did not oppose him and replied that he was merely proposing to "substitute a democratic for an autocratic basis."[54]

On 26 May, the Allies offered Kolchak support, provided he agreed to a number of political conditions. The Allies blamed the Soviet government for its alleged refusal to suspend hostilities while negotiations or relief work were proceeding. They stated that they wanted the Russian people to resume control of their own national affairs through the Constituent Assembly. The experiences of the last twelve months had convinced them that that goal would not be possible to achieve through cooperation with the Soviet government. Therefore, they offered to assist the government of Admiral Kolchak with deliveries of munitions and food, provided the Allies received from him "definite guarantees" about his political objectives. The Allied conditions included the reinstatement of the Constituent Assembly, new elections on all governmental levels, and the promise that the old tsarist political and social system would not be revived.[55]

On 4 June, Kolchak accepted most of these conditions but refused to reinstate the Constituent Assembly, arguing that it was elected during the time of Soviet rule. The Allies considered Kolchak's answer satisfactory and informed him on 12 June that they were willing to extend the support set forth in their original letter. On 24 June, Wilson authorized $5 million for relief of the Russian civilian population and restoration of railway traffic in Siberia.[56]

In the following weeks, there was confusion among State Department officials in Washington about the diplomatic implications of the exchange of notes between the Allies and Kolchak. On 25 June, Wilson made it clear that the telegram to Kolchak did not imply political recognition as the de facto government at the present time.[57]

In June 1919, the United States gave up the policy of neutrality in favor of supporting one civil war faction. General Graves had recommended such a step in May if the administration desired to aid Kolchak's fight against the Bolsheviks. Despite the refusal to grant him diplomatic recognition, the United States supported him by delivering weapons.[58]

Despite the Allied intervention into the Russian civil war and the support for Kolchak, it became increasingly clear in late summer 1919 that he would suffer a defeat. In the fall, the Red Army conquered all large towns along the Trans-Siberian Railway. The Soviet military successes posed the danger of an imminent clash with American troops. In this situation in late December 1919, Wilson decided to withdraw the Expeditionary Army from Siberia.[59]

Wilson's decisions to join the Allied intervention and to support Kolchak were two of the most controversial measures the president took during his time in office. Only two weeks before he endorsed aid to Kolchak, he had declared in a meeting of the Council of Four: "Our government does not have confidence in Admiral Kolchak, who is supported by France and England." On 10 May, Wilson told Nicolai V. Chaikovskii, a member of the Russian political council,[60] who was in Paris in 1919 to lobby for Allied support for the anti-Bolsheviks, that he was not "entirely satisfied that the leadership of Kolchak was calculated to preserve what ought to be preserved of the new order of things in Russia." He feared that it would result in a "policy of reaction and military power." In early May, Wilson rejected the idea of increasing the number of U.S. troops in Russia and of supporting Kolchak. The president's subsequent change of mind later the same month has been analyzed by political and medical historians. Medical historian Bert Park, for example, has found conclusive evidence that "by mid-March 1919, a recognizable syndrome compatible with multi-infarct dementia had emerged." During the final phase of the Paris Peace Conference Wilson repeatedly complained of weariness.[61] But a medical analysis cannot answer the question of why Wilson decided to support Kolchak. Political historians, however, are split over the question of Wilson's goal in supporting him. Historian Levin argues that Wilson considered Kolchak a representative of Russian liberalism: "Wilson was perfectly prepared to extend assistance to those portions of Russia where indigenous anti-communist forces appeared to be potentially capable of establishing the basis for a non-Bolshevik liberal order." The president hoped that "a liberal-nationalist Siberia would eventually rejoin a non-Bolshevik and pro-Allied regime throughout Russia. During 1919, the anti-Bolshevik Siberian leader Admiral Kolchak carried Allied and American hopes in this regard."[62] Levin considered Wilson's decisions to intervene in Russia and to support Kolchak as serving the same purpose. The Bolshevik rule was to be substituted by a liberal government. But Levin does not demonstrate whether the intervention had any purpose other than eliminating a leftist dictatorship. While Wilson repeatedly denounced the Soviets, he never publicly called Kolchak an example of Russian liberalism or democracy. In fact, Wilson criticized Kolchak on various occasions before he decided to support him. Moreover, it seems unjustifiable to speak of a Russian "liberalism" in 1919. "Liberalism" only appears to be a euphemism for "anti-Bolshevik" and "anti-Japanese." Historian Betty M. Unterberger follows this line of interpretation. She points out that the position of the American troops in Russia had become untenable in the spring of 1919 because of potential conflicts with the Allies and with the Bolsheviks. A unilateral American withdrawal from Russia "would have left Japan in virtual control of northern Manchuria and Eastern Siberia." In order to prevent the Japanese government from becoming the dominant power in Siberia, "Wilson finally agreed to offer support to Kolchak, although he insisted that democratic pledges be secured from him."[63] By supporting Kolchak, Wilson reaffirmed the *realpolitik* goal of maintaining Allied unity and saved Siberia from Bolshevik and from Japanese domination.

Wilson only considered aiding Kolchak after it had become obvious that without foreign assistance his armies would be defeated by the Bolsheviks because of a lack of popular support. The president regarded Kolchak as anti-Bolshevik and anti-Japanese, and in contrast to other local resistance groups, Kolchak did not favor independence for peripheral non-Russian territories but desired to achieve a united Russia. It was not Wilson's goal to lead the Allied troops to a military victory over the Bolsheviks. He considered the support for Kolchak as part of a wider ideological confrontation of nationalist forces with the Soviets. Wilson's and Kolchak's views regarding Russian unity even under the violation of the right of national self-determination of non-Russian people were similar. Kolchak's defeat, therefore, was the defeat of Wilson's Russian policy. For the sake of this policy, a number of promising democratic—but separatist—movements had been sacrificed in the conflict between Russian national self-determination versus "Russia One and Indivisible."

Kolchak's defeat was not the only setback Wilson suffered following the Paris Peace Conference. In July 1919, he presented the proposed Treaty of Versailles to the Senate for approval. Many senators expressed concern about certain aspects of the agreement, such as the combination of a peace treaty with Germany with automatic U.S. membership in the League of Nations. Republican isolationists such as William E. Borah of Idaho, leader of the "irreconcilable" faction in the United States Senate, rejected the concept of collective security arrangements. Senator Henry Cabot Lodge of Massachusetts, chairman of the Senate Foreign Relations Committee, and former Secretary of State Elihu Root held strong reservations about the treaty. They did not reject the idea of joining an international political organization, but objected that membership in the League, as proposed by the president, would restrict American freedom of political action. Lodge complained that Article X of the League Covenant bound members to "respect and preserve as against external aggression the territorial integrity and existing political independence" of all member states. That provision would compel the United States to use force to "guarantee the territorial integrity of the far-flung British empire."[64]

On 4 March 1919, thirty-seven senators, enough to reject the peace treaty, demanded amendments and reservations to the proposed treaty, designed to recognize the provisions of the Monroe Doctrine and to guarantee the sole responsibility of Congress in deploying U.S. troops in international military conflicts. Wilson rejected all amendments and reservations to the Versailles Treaty and criticized Republican senators for advocating isolationism in America.[65] The president decided to take his cause directly to the American people. In September, he tirelessly lobbied for the original agreement in speeches around the United States. During a pro-League address in Pueblo, Colorado, on 25 September, Wilson fell seriously ill, and on 2 October he suffered a debilitating stroke. On 19 March 1920, Wilson witnessed the Senate rejection of both the Treaty of Versailles and of U.S. membership in the League of Nations.[66]

Wilson's diplomatic efforts during the Paris Peace Conference to establish democracy in Russia failed. His proposal that all Russian civil war groups meet at the island of Principo was rejected by the anti-Soviet groups. Wilson's reaction to this and other initiatives showed that he was not willing to accept Bolshevik rule as the legitimate Russian government. Instead, Wilson was looking for something that was not there: a democratic group that would give Russia a government not unlike that of the United States. When the time to search for such a group was almost over at the end of the Paris Peace Conference, Wilson endorsed the one anti-Soviet group that, while not democratic, at least appeared able to defeat the Bolsheviks militarily. Kolchak's defeat also was the defeat of Wilson's Russian policy.

5

National Self-Determination Versus "Russia One and Indivisible"

In his Fourteen Points speech of January 1918, President Wilson defined the goals of his Russian policy as restoring Russian unity and safeguarding the Russian people's right of national self-determination. Wilson understood self-determination to mean the withdrawal of all foreign troops from Russia and the establishment of a single democratic government there. That program could only be instituted after Germany was defeated and had withdrawn from Russian soil. That goal was accomplished in November 1918. Furthermore, the Bolshevik rule in Russia had to be replaced by a democratic government. Wilson never wavered in his expectation of an eventual victory of the democratic forces in Russia. After the Allied military intervention had proved ineffective in creating a single democratic government in Russia, Wilson faced a dilemma: which of his two goals should receive priority? Should the "idea" of a united Russian state be kept alive to make a future democratic Russia possible? Under that policy, the Bolsheviks could consolidate their power as the de facto rulers of Russia, including the Baltic provinces, Siberia, the Ukraine, and other areas. Or should the United States support non-Russian people in their quest for independence from socialist Russia? That policy would lead to the splitting up of Russia into numerous independent states.[1]

After the end of the First World War, the Russian problem lost most of its urgency for the U.S. government. Germany was defeated, socialist revolutions in Western Europe failed, and Russia, weakened by the civil war and poor harvests, no longer appeared an imminent political danger. With no Allied political and military pressure on him, Wilson was again free to devise a genuine Russian policy. That policy was again dominated by ideological considerations and expectations of a future united democratic Russia.

During the Paris Peace Conference, the Baltic provinces Estonia, Latvia, and Lithuania, the Ukraine, Armenia, and Azerbaijan sought international recognition as sovereign states. They sent delegations to Paris to lobby the Western statesmen to help them in their struggle to maintain their newly won independence. The Soviet government made it clear that it accepted the secession of non-Russian republics from Soviet Russia. Lenin's proposal of April 1919 submitted to William C. Bullitt implied the splitting up of Russian territory along the lines of de facto control.[2]

Among the members of the American delegation to the Paris Peace Conference, Harvard University history professor Robert H. Lord and Samuel Morison, both specialists in Eastern European affairs, and Colonel House strongly recommended the recognition of the sovereignty of the Baltic provinces. Lord and Morison believed that neither the Bolsheviks nor the counterrevolutionary forces, such as Admiral Kolchak's, would turn Russia into a democracy. The best chances for democratization were in the more Western-oriented and more highly developed three Baltic republics. A potential democratic development there would be jeopardized by tying them to Soviet Russia. Lord and Morison recommended that "[c]ollective recognition by the Associated Governments of the Provisional Governments of Latvia, Lithuania and Estonia should no longer be delayed." The two scholars acknowledged the importance of the Baltic provinces for Russia. A large part of Russian imports and exports were handled at the Baltic seaports. But they believed that it would be possible to accommodate Russian and Baltic interests. "Some reservations to protect Russia's right and interests in these countries must be included in their recognition." Colonel House, too, advocated the breakup of Russia. He wrote on 19 September 1918 that Russia was "too big and homogeneous for the safety of the world." And: "I would like to see Siberia a separate republic, and European Russia divided into three parts."[3]

A diametrically opposed opinion was expressed by Professor Samuel Harper of the University of Chicago and by John Spargo in his influential book *Russia As an American Problem*. Harper, one of the foremost Soviet scholars in the United States at the time, was one of the first to urge a policy of keeping Russia united. In a memorandum written shortly after the October Revolution, he emphasized that liberals and moderate socialists like Pavel Miliukov and Alexander Kerensky were fighting hard to preserve the integrity of the state. They were the constructive forces to which the administration should look. The United States "must not recognize the independence of any of the districts such as Finland or the Ukraine until we are quite certain that the declaration of independence is genuine." Harper continued with a clear endorsement of maintaining Russian unity: "Though we are also the champions of the rights of small nations, we must nevertheless realize that we might be contributing to the destruction of small nationalities, at the hand of Germany, by premature action, tending to recognize temporary conditions of a period of readjustment."[4]

Harper was aware that keeping Russian unity intact would serve the interests of the Bolsheviks. He accepted that fact for two reasons. First, Germany would be the main beneficiary of a divided Russia. Second, he doubted that the Lenin government would stay in power for long. The Bolsheviks, he wrote, might be able to maintain themselves in power for some time. In the end, however, they would fail, though the cost to Russia would have been enormous.[5]

Spargo, a socialist who had advocated American entry into the war in 1917, also rejected the idea of splitting up the Russian territory. His argument was that, by breaking up its territory, Russia would lose some of its most valuable provinces, the highly developed Baltic states with their history of trading with Northern Europe and oil-rich Azerbaijan. Only a united Russia could ever be economically prosperous. Out of the countless new states, on the other hand, many would be too small to be successful: "With the exception of Poland and Finland . . . the splitting up of European Russia is to be regarded as a retrogressive step, injurious to Russia and to the seceding states."[6]

Spargo, whose ideas were influential with the Wilson administration, particularly with Lansing's successor as secretary of state, Bainbridge Colby, considered the Bolsheviks opportunists. He believed that economic pressure from the West could induce considerable reforms in Russia. He, therefore, rejected the idea of granting the Bolsheviks diplomatic recognition but advocated a resumption of trade with them and a rejection of the Baltic pleas for recognition of their independence. The main goal must be to democratize a united Russia: "Any attempt to dismember Russia in such a manner, for the protection of western Europe, would unite all factions in Russia against it. There will cease to be a majority in Russia struggling to overthrow the Bolshevik minority."[7]

During his remaining months in office, President Wilson's policy was directed toward maintaining Russian unity as it was at the outset of the First World War. He told a delegation from the province of Azerbaijan who sought international recognition for its province that the peace conference did not intend to dissolve the world into little nation-states. Secretary Lansing told a Ukrainian delegation in late June 1919 that the United States did not support independence for the Ukraine, but that it "was in favor of a single Russia in which various portions could have a certain degree of autonomy."[8]

Wilson and Lansing limited the right of national self-determination for the non-Russian people of the former tsarist empire. That policy was based on their belief in an imminent collapse of the Soviet regime and the establishment of a democratic government there. On 5 November 1920, on the eve of the third anniversary of the October Revolution, Wilson wrote to Lloyd George: "As to Russia, I cannot but feel that Bolshevism would have burned out long ago if let alone, and that no practical and permanent settlement involving Russian territory and rights can be arrived at until the great Russian people can express themselves through a recognized government of their own choice."[9] That was again the ideological Wilson who criticized his own aberration from the right course by supporting the intervention in 1918 instead of letting the Russians "wallow in anarchy" for a while.

A future democratic Russia, in Wilson's eyes, had the right to determine its own fate without outside interference. The Russian republics were economically unstable and were in danger of becoming dependent on other countries. Secretary Lansing wrote in December 1919, at a time when Kolchak's defeat in the civil war had become obvious: "The American Government will give no support to the view that the dismemberment of Russia should be encouraged because a united Russia will be a menace to Europe. . . . [I]t is believed that a divided Russia not able to cope with existing Japanese territorial ambition or a possible revival of German imperialism would be by far a greater menace to the British Empire than would be a united, democratic Russia, well able to defend itself, but not disposed to attack."[10] Lansing still considered a democratic development very likely. But neither Wilson nor Lansing ever reflected on how democracy could develop in a state without any previous democratic traditions. In his public statements about Russia after the Paris Peace Conference, Wilson repeatedly condemned the Bolsheviks for ideological reasons. He considered them representatives of a kind of government that was diametrically opposed to American principles. He never believed that any of the counterrevolutionary civil war parties satisfied democratic claims. On 6 September 1919, Wilson said in a speech in Kansas City:

[I]t doesn't make any difference what kind of minority governs you, if it is a minority . . . the men who are now largely in control of the affairs of Russia represent nobody but themselves. . . . They have no mandate from anybody. There are only thirty-four of them, I am told, and there were more than thirty-four men who used to control the destinies of Europe from Wilhelmstrasse. There is a closer monopoly of power in Petrograd and Moscow than there ever was in Berlin.[11]

Wilson interpreted the October Revolution as a victory of an authoritarian minority over the Russian population's wishes for a democratic government. U.S. policy, however, was limited to ignoring the Bolsheviks' claim of exerting governmental power over a united Russia.

After the conclusion of the Paris Peace Conference in June 1919, Russian affairs played only a minor role during the remaining months of the Wilson administration. In July and August, the British and French governments urged the president to join them in imposing a complete economic blockade of Russia. Wilson, however, rejected their appeal because the United States was not officially at war with the Soviets. Instead, he encouraged the British and French to request other states to refrain from dealing with the Bolshevik regime.[12]

The president's main political goal was to convince the United States Senate and the American people of the importance of the Treaty of Versailles. After Wilson suffered a stroke in late September that greatly handicapped his ability to work, Russian problems almost completely disappeared from his agenda. It was only during the Russo-Polish War of April through October 1920 that Russian affairs again briefly moved to the center of the Wilson administration's attention.

Poland was discontented with its borders as they were drawn at the Paris Peace Conference and sought to annex parts of Lithuania that had been Polish territories from the sixteenth century until the Polish partitions in the eighteenth century when they became part of the Russian Empire. The Paris Peace Conference could do little to redraw the Russo-Polish borders because there were no Russian negotiators at Paris who could agree to a new boundary. Besides those practical problems, members of the American delegation were aware that it would be impossible to solve such a long-running territorial dispute at the conference. As Robert Lord put it, Allied diplomats were anxious to "keep the aspirations of the new ally, Poland, within limits that would not irrevocably antagonize the old ally that might some day be won back—Russia."[13] Dissatisfied with the Western support of their territorial claims, the Poles used the Russian internal weakness following the Revolution and the civil war to annex the Ukraine and parts of Lithuania and Byelorussia.

During the Russian civil war, the Polish government under Marshal Joseph Pilsudski remained neutral. When the Soviet victory became clear, Polish troops invaded the Ukraine in the spring of 1920. In early May they occupied the capital Kiev. The challenge of a foreign invasion caused nationalistic forces in Russia to support the Bolsheviks, who at that time commanded the only military force in Russia able to resist the invader. General Aleksei A. Brusilov, the last supreme commander of the army under the tsar, urged all former officers to join the Red Army in its fight against the Polish invaders. After initial Polish military successes, the Red Army drove back the invader. In June, General Mikhail N. Tukhachevskii recaptured Kiev; by late July, the Soviets had forced the Poles behind the previous Polish-Russian frontiers. In August, the Polish army, aided by French military advisers and supplied with French equipment, counterattacked. By that time, however, the Poles had given up plans to annex the Ukraine. In the treaty of Riga, signed in March 1921, only small parts of Byelorussia and the Ukraine became Polish territories.[14]

The Russo-Polish controversy was unwelcome news for the Wilson administration. It proved that the postwar order that was decided on in Paris was volatile. Only months after the peace treaty had been signed, states again resorted to military aggressions to solve border disputes. For Wilson, the Russo-Polish War also meant a personal defeat. The president had agreed to hold the peace conference following World War I without German or Russian participation. Essential border disputes could therefore not be settled with all parties involved participating. The first postconference conflict developed in an area where the dominant states had been excluded from the negotiations. But Wilson's personal defeat went even further. In points 6 and 13 of his Fourteen Points speech of January 1918, he had specifically guaranteed both Russia's and Poland's territorial integrity. His postwar grand scheme appeared threatened. In 1920, Wilson could not again take part in another foreign military intervention to settle a European conflict. But at the same time he abhorred the possibility of a Bolshevik success in the war against Poland.

The U.S. policy in the Russo-Polish War was to maintain neutrality. The administration refused appealing to the Russian government for a peaceful settlement because that implied recognition of the Bolsheviks as the de facto Russian government. In response to a Polish inquiry in January 1920 about how to respond to Soviet offers of peace, Secretary Lansing informed the American minister in Poland, Hugh S. Gibson, that the American refusal to communicate with the Soviets did not mean that the administration would provide Poland with economic assistance if it too refused to enter into negotiations with the Bolsheviks.[15]

In mid-July, Gibson asked Secretary of State Bainbridge Colby to clarify the American position on the Russo-Polish War. Colby, a former corporate lawyer and member of the United States Shipping Board who had only limited experience in foreign affairs, had succeeded Lansing as secretary of state in February 1920.[16] The Polish government, Gibson wrote, had made mistakes in its reactions to Soviet proposals to end the war in January 1920. Those mistakes, however, were "due in part to conflicting policies of the

Allied Powers." The United States had told the Polish government that, in Gibson's words, the United States was not in a position to offer advice, but that the "failure to advise the conclusion of peace must not be construed as a tacit promise of material support." The United States, in other words, did not recommend a Polish peace treaty with the Bolsheviks in January 1920, but made it clear that it would not support Pilsudski. Great Britain, on the other hand, had advised immediate peace with the Bolsheviks, France had recommended "dilatory tactics in the hope of an internal collapse of the Bolshevik regime," and Italy had favored "offensive warfare." In that situation, the Poles had chosen the "unwise course" of continued warfare.

Gibson asked the State Department for a statement by President Wilson directed toward the Polish people reaffirming the American friendship. Wilson rejected Gibson's recommendation of a personal intervention on 20 July because he believed that the time had passed when a presidential message could solve the Russo-Polish dispute. When Wilson received a note from Polish Prime Minister Kazimierz Lubomirski on 31 July, he refused to answer it himself and instructed Colby to draft a reply.[17]

On 5 August Alessandro Mariani, a secretary of the Italian embassy in Washington, inquired about the American policy toward Soviet Russia and the Russo-Polish War. The following day, Wilson, Colby, and Under Secretary of State Norman Davis met at the White House to discuss a response to the Italian inquiry. In a diplomatic note to the Italian ambassador to Washington, Baron Camilio Romano Avezzano, on 10 August, later to be called the "Colby Note," the administration drafted a position paper that became the rationale for American nonrecognition policy of the Soviet Union for the next thirteen years.

The note advocated Russo-Polish armistice negotiations but rejected the idea of an international conference with Soviet participation because that implied the recognition of the Bolshevik regime and the dismemberment of Russia. It went on to call the United States the guarantor of Russia's territorial interests. Until a united democratic government could be installed there, "the United States feels that friendship and honor require that Russia's interest must be generously protected and that, as far as possible, all decisions of vital importance to it, and especially those concerning its sovereignty over the territory of the former Russian Empire, be held in abeyance." The administration recalled its refusals to grant recognition to a number of groups claiming the right to secede from Russia, such as the Lithuanian National Council, whose request was rejected on 15 October 1919. Only the legitimate government could decide about territorial changes in Russia. The current rulers did not govern with the consent of the people. Instead, the existing regime was based on the "negation of every principle of honor and good faith . . . in short, of every principle upon which it is possible to base harmonious and trustful relations." The U.S. government would favor a joint European note denouncing any changes in the Russian territorial status: "Such a declaration presupposes the withdrawal of all foreign troops from the territory embraced in these boundaries, and in the opinion of this government should be accompanied by the announcement that no transgression by Poland, Finland or any other Power, of the line so drawn and proclaimed will be permitted."[18]

In the Russo-Polish conflict, the Wilson administration attempted to defend the compromise between the territorial interests of both countries that was reached at the Paris Peace Conference. Wilson's role as protector of Russian interests, therefore, proved to have a stabilizing influence on the Bolshevik regime because no foreign intervention forces could count on American support. Wilson desired to maintain Russian unity in hopes that it would some day lead to a democratic Russia. The former Russian provinces that had gained independence, therefore, were forced to enter into relations with the Bolsheviks.[19]

The Soviet government reacted to the Colby Note with indignation and open hostility. Soviet Foreign Minister Georgi Chicherin wrote that the American note insisted on the territorial inviolability of the former Russian territories, except for Poland, Finland, and Armenia. The independence of those states would be permissible because Russia had annexed them by force. The United States would not grant the right to secession to the Georgian, Azerbaijan, and other peoples. This distinction between the various nationalities that had come under the rule of the former Russian Empire was "incomprehensible," and in "all probability it is based on the American Government's ignorance of the real facts of the national inter-relations in eastern Europe."[20]

Why did Wilson and Colby still cling to a Russian policy that was an anachronism in the eyes of countless contemporaries and many historians? Historian Daniel Smith, for example, wrote that the Colby Note "formalized a policy of non-recognition that was to become increasingly unrealistic as the Soviet government solidified its authority." Joan Hoff-Wilson noted that by "ideologically holding out for an entirely democratic, capitalistic Russia, the United States pursued a policy that resulted in the loss of the entire nation to Western political and economic traditions." In the debate about Russia in the United States and Western Europe between supporters and enemies of the Soviet regime, Wilson occupied a middle position. This attitude reflected two considerations: He estimated that in order to defeat the Bolsheviks an army of at least 50,000 thoroughly trained and well-equipped men would be necessary. None of the Russian counterrevolutionary groups would come close to that figure. And no Western European country was able or willing to wage war against Russia in 1919 or 1920. It was impossible to imagine that the United States Congress would have declared war on Russia if Wilson had asked it to do so. The president distanced himself from plans to conquer Russia that were drafted by English and French delegates at the Paris Peace Conference.[21] But he refused to recognize the Bolshevik rule, because, as historian Christopher Lasch has pointed out, like all American liberals, he could not accept the viability of the undemocratic Bolshevik Revolution without denying his rooted faith in worldwide progress. Under the precepts of liberalism, Bolshevism—logically—could not last.[22]

Conclusions: Between Ideology and *Realpolitik*

For it is clear that in fundamental theory socialism and democracy are almost if not quite one and the same. They both rest upon the absolute right of the community to determine its own destiny and that of its members. Men as communities are supreme over men as individuals. Limits of wisdom and convenience to the public control there may be: limits of principle there are, upon strict analysis, none.

The difference between democracy and socialism is not an essential difference, but only a practical difference—is a difference of *organization* and *policy*, not a difference of primary motive. Democracy has not undertaken the tasks which socialists clamour to have undertaken; but it refrains from them . . . for lack of adequate organization and suitable hardihood.

— Woodrow Wilson, "Socialism and Democracy"[1]

It was a strange fate of history that within two weeks in late January and early February 1924 both Wilson and Lenin, the two great ideological antipodes of the early twentieth century, died from the effects of a stroke. For almost three generations, historians have studied their ideological differences, the struggle between liberal democracy and socialism. From the point of view of the post–Cold War late twentieth century, however, Wilson and Lenin appear more similar in their struggles than either man might have ever imagined. They were astute observers of the exploitation and growing inequality of living conditions between rich and poor in the industrializing states that called for relief. Both Wilson and Lenin keenly diagnosed the problems and agreed to a large extent about the political and economic grievances of their time. They differed, however, in the remedies they advocated.

Wilson's speeches and writings from the early years of the twentieth century reflected his convictions that economic and political developments in the United States since the start of industrialization had not always been for the better. He sensed that Americans had become more and more alienated by those economic developments. In an early essay on "Socialism and Democracy" (1887), he wrote:

Many affairs of life which were once easily to be handled by individuals have now become so entangled amongst the complexities of international trade relations, so confused by the multiplicity of news-voices, or so hoisted into the winds of speculation that only powerful combinations of wealth and influence can compass them. Corporations grow on every hand, and on every hand not only swallow and overawe individuals but also compete with governments. The contest is no longer between government and individuals; it is now between governments and dangerous combinations and individuals. Here is a monstrously changed aspect of the social world.[2]

Similar statements can be found in speeches during the Progressive Era, particularly while Wilson was campaigning for the presidency in 1912. In one of his campaign speeches, "The Old Order Changeth," published in a collection of campaign speeches under the programmatic title, *The New Freedom*, he said that "we are all caught in a great economic system which is heartless. The modern corporation is not engaged in business as an individual. When we deal with it, we deal with an impersonal element, an immaterial piece of society." In another speech, "What Is Progress," he was even more explicit: "By tyranny, as we now fight it, we mean control of the law, of legislation and adjudication, by organizations which do not represent the people, by means which are private and selfish. We mean, specifically, the conduct of our affairs and the shaping of our legislation in the interest of special bodies of capital and those who organize their use."[3]

Wilson was a harsh critic of the economic organization and political condition: "Why are we in the presence, why are we at the threshold, of a revolution? Because we are profoundly disturbed by the influences which we see reigning in the determination of our public life and policy." The United States was on the eve of a "silent revolution, whereby America will insist upon recovering in practice those ideals which she has always professed, upon securing a government devoted to the general interest and not to special interests." Wilson saw the political freedom of the American people challenged by the concentration of economic power in the hands of a few industrialists. But in contrast to Lenin who advocated the nationalization of the means of production, Wilson sought a greater role for smaller private units in national economic affairs. Political freedom to him depended on the ownership of the means of production by individuals. Both the big impersonal corporations and the socialists challenged that right. To Wilson, the primary function of government, as historian Samuel P. Hays wrote, "was to destroy roadblocks to opportunity, not to provide positive services for the American people." His vision for America was that of the past, of the country's heritage of politically interested and independently producing citizens.[4]

Neither Wilson's vision of an economy based on independent small producers nor Lenin's goal of a global classless society governs the international political economy in the late twentieth century. This allows a more detached view on their conflict than was possible during the Cold War years.

Both Wilson and Lenin considered themselves strict adherents to moral systems and set out to conduct an ideological foreign policy. In their dealings with allies and opponents, however, they soon discovered the need for a *realpolitik* approach to current problems. After an initial revolutionary outburst in the months immediately after the October Revolution, Soviet policy, both domestic and foreign, turned into a pragmatic response to acute international conflicts when the hope of socialist revolutions in other states remained unfulfilled.

President Wilson's ideological rhetoric throughout the period of the Russian Revolution has led historians to believe that his major political decisions were determined almost exclusively by moral considerations. In fact, however, it appears that, while Wilson used moral arguments to justify all important decisions, considerations of *realpolitik* strongly affected his thinking. Initially, he rejected a military intervention in the Russian civil war as dangerous, costly, and, above all, unnecessary because the Bolshevik rule would only be temporary. He never reversed that opinion but accepted U.S. participation in the intervention after persistent pressure from the Allies. His goal was to maintain the unity of the democratic forces during the war. Nevertheless, Wilson justified the decision to intervene with moral arguments. When the pressure to maintain Allied unity abated after the end of the world war and the counterrevolutionary forces in Russia proved incapable of overthrowing the Bolsheviks, Wilson returned to his initial ideological concept of not dealing with and not fighting against the Soviets.

The Wilson who agreed to the Allied intervention in the summer of 1918 and the Wilson who sought to maintain Russian territorial unity one year later at the Paris Peace Conference almost seem like two different people. It appears futile to interpret his Russian policies from 1917 through 1920 as directed toward achieving one overriding goal. The hotly contested question among Western historians of whether Wilson intervened in Russia to defeat the Bolsheviks, to help the liberals, or to keep the Germans and/or the Japanese out of the country is of only secondary importance. More important for the understanding of Wilson's policy is that for ideological reasons he did not consider any intervention there necessary, and he only joined the Allied endeavor to satisfy a practical need for unity.

Wilson never gave up his ideological opposition to the Soviets and never lost faith in the Russian people. He hoped that they would sooner or later establish a democratic government without any outside interference as Americans had done 150 years earlier and as the Russians themselves had done without outside help in March 1917. The tragedy of Wilson's Russian policy was that there was no historical basis for a unified democratic Russia. Unlike Americans who had accepted the idea of many nationalities living within one state, the Russian experience was that of an empire. Russia, too, contained within its borders many nationalities. Non-Russians, however, considered the Russians not as compatriots but as conquerors and exploiters, and therefore sought independence. It is indicative of the failure of Wilson's policy that as soon as the Soviet Union threw off the communist dictatorship in the early

1990s, the non-Russian people immediately sought the right to secede. This time the democratic government under President Boris Yeltsin granted their wish. Wilson's vision of a multinational democratic Russia within the borders of the tsarist empire was the projection of the American experience to the Eurasian continent, but it was in no way based on the realities of Eastern European national antagonisms.

Notes

INTRODUCTION

1. Woodrow Wilson, "The Road Away from Revolution," *The Atlantic Monthly* 132 (1923): 145–46. Also printed in Arthur S. Link, ed., *The Papers of Woodrow Wilson (PWW)* (68 vols., Princeton, N.J.: Princeton University Press, 1966–93), vol. 68, p. 393. On the reasons why Wilson wrote the article about the Russian Revolution, see August Heckscher, *Woodrow Wilson* (New York: Charles Scribner's Sons, 1991), pp. 665–67 and Gene Smith, *When the Cheering Stopped: The Last Years of Woodrow Wilson* (New York: Time Inc., 1966), pp. 211–12.

2. *PWW*, vol. 68, pp. 394–95.

3. Ibid., p. 394.

4. Lloyd E. Ambrosius, *Wilsonian Statecraft: Theory and Practice of Liberal Internationalism During World War I* (Wilmington, Del.: Scholarly Resources, 1991), pp. 10–13; John M. Thompson, *Russia, Bolshevism, and the Versailles Peace* (Princeton, N.J.: Princeton University Press, 1966), p. 40.

5. George F. Kennan, *Russia Leaves the War* (New York: W.W. Norton, 1984), pp. 12–13, 28, 33; James K. Libbey, "The American-Russian Chamber of Commerce," *Diplomatic History* 9 (1985): 234.

6. It was called "provisional" because one of its tasks was to convene a constituent assembly that would decide on procedures to elect a regular government. Neither the prime minister nor any of the Provisional Government's cabinet members were elected to their new offices.

Instead, the government derived its authority indirectly from its links with the Duma. See Leonard Shapiro, *1917: The Russian Revolution and the Origins of Present-Day Communism* (Hounslow: Maurice Temple Smith, 1984), p. 56.

7. *PWW,* vol. 41, p. 524.

8. Trotsky as quoted in Isaac Deutscher, *The Prophet Armed: Trotsky, 1879–1921* (New York: Oxford University Press, 1954), p. 246; Walther Rathenau, *Nach der Flut* (1919), as quoted in Arno Mayer, *Wilson vs. Lenin: Political Origins of the New Diplomacy, 1917–1918* (Cleveland: Meridian, 1964), p. 31.

9. Wilson Address to a Labor Convention in Buffalo, 12 November 1917, *PWW,* vol. 45, p. 14; Meeting of the Council of Ten, 16 January 1919, *PWW,* vol. 54, pp. 102–3.

10. British Foreign Office Memorandum, included in Ambassador Walter H. Page to Secretary Lansing, 29 December 1917, Department of State, *Papers Relating to the Foreign Relations of the United States (FRUS),* 1918, Russia (3 vols., Washington, D.C.: Government Printing Office [GPO], 1931–32), vol. 1, pp. 330–31; Louis Fischer, *Russia's Road from War to Peace: Soviet Foreign Relations, 1917–1941* (New York: Harper and Row, 1969), pp. 14–16; Lansing to General Tasker H. Bliss, 2 February 1918, Tasker H. Bliss Papers, Library of Congress; Heckscher, *Woodrow Wilson,* pp. 463–65; Jan Willem Schulte-Nordholt, *Woodrow Wilson: A Life for World Peace* (Berkeley: University of California Press, 1991), p. 308.

11. Arthur S. Link, *Woodrow Wilson: Revolution, War, and Peace* (Arlington Heights, Ill.: Harlan Davidson, 1979), pp 6–7.

12. N. Gordon Levin, *Woodrow Wilson and World Politics: America's Response to War and Revolution* (New York: Oxford University Press, 1968), p. 8. Emphasis in original.

13. Randolph S. Bourne, "The Collapse of American Strategy" (August 1917), as quoted in Lloyd E. Ambrosius, *Woodrow Wilson and the American Diplomatic Tradition: The Treaty Fight in Perspective* (New York: Cambridge University Press, 1987), pp. 33–34.

CHAPTER 1

1. George F. Kennan, *The Decision to Intervene* (New York: W.W. Norton, 1984), p. 13.

2. Arthur S. Link, ed., *The Papers of Woodrow Wilson (PWW)* (68 vols., Princeton, N.J.: Princeton University Press, 1966–93), vol. 41, pp. 520, 526; Robert H. Ferrell, *Woodrow Wilson and World War I, 1917–1921* (New York: Harper and Row, 1985), p. 3.

3. William J. Bryan, *The Memoirs of William Jennings Bryan* (Philadelphia: John C. Winston, 1925), pp. 398–400, 406–7; Louis W. Koenig, *Bryan: A Political Biography of William Jennings Bryan* (New York: G. P. Putnam's Sons, 1971); Akira Iriye, *The Globalizing of America, 1914–1945* (Cambridge: Cambridge University Press, 1993), pp. 21–26; Richard Challener, "William Jennings Bryan," in Norman Graebner, ed., *An Uncertain Tradition: American Secretaries of State in the Twentieth Century* (Westport, Conn.: Greenwood Press, 1961), pp. 95–100.

4. Lansing Diary, 3 December 1916, Robert F. Lansing Papers, Library of Congress, Washington, D.C.; *New York Times*, 22 December 1916, *PWW*, vol. 40, p. 307n. 1; Daniel M. Smith, "Robert Lansing," in Graebner, *Uncertain Tradition*, pp. 101–27; Daniel M. Smith, *Robert Lansing and American Neutrality, 1914–1917* (Berkeley: University of California Press, 1958), p. 168.

5. *PWW*, vol. 38, p. 531; N. Gordon Levin, *Woodrow Wilson and World Politics: America's Response to War and Revolution* (New York: Oxford University Press, 1968), pp. 32–33.

6. *PWW*, vol. 38, p. 531.

7. Ibid., vol. 40, p. 274.

8. Ibid., vol. 40, pp. 535–36.

9. Arthur S. Link, *Wilson*, vol. 5, *Campaigns for Progressivism and Peace, 1916–1917* (Princeton, N.J.: Princeton University Press, 1965), p. 411; Wilson to Gavit, 29 January 1917, *PWW*, vol. 41, p. 55.

10. August Heckscher, *Woodrow Wilson* (New York: Charles Scribner's Sons, 1991), pp. 423–24; Daniel M. Smith, *The Great Departure: The United States and World War I* (New York: Knopf, 1965), pp. 72–74.

11. United States Department of State, *Papers Relating to the Foreign Relations of the United States (FRUS)*, The Lansing Papers, 1914–20 (2 vols., Washington, D.C.: GPO, 1940), vol. 1, p. 421.

12. Wilson Speech before the Senate, 3 February 1917, *PWW*, vol. 41, p. 111; Wilson to Cobb, as quoted in John M. Cooper, *The Warrior and the Priest: Woodrow Wilson and Theodore Roosevelt* (Cambridge, Mass.: Belknap, 1983), pp. 319–20.

13. Heckscher, *Wilson*, p. 427; Woodrow Wilson, *PWW*, vol. 51, p. 131; Woodrow Wilson, "The Bible and Progress," Address, 7 May 1911, *PWW*, vol. 23, p. 20.

14. Wilson Address on 10 July 1916, *PWW*, vol. 37, p. 387.

15. Lloyd E. Ambrosius, *Wilsonian Statecraft: Theory and Practice of Liberal Internationalism During World War I* (Wilmington, Del.: Scholarly Resources, 1991), p. 11; Address to a Joint Session of Congress, 2 April 1917, *PWW*, vol. 41, pp. 519–27; Wilson's Memorial Day Address, Arlington Cemetery, *PWW*, vol. 42, p. 423; State of the Union Address, *PWW*, vol. 45, p. 196.

16. Wilson to House, 22 August 1917, *PWW*, vol. 44, p. 33; Levin, *Wilson and World Politics*, pp. 52–55; Thomas Knock, *To End All Wars: Woodrow Wilson and the Quest for a New World Order* (New York: Oxford University Press, 1992), p. 145; Kendrick A. Clements, *Woodrow Wilson, World Statesman* (Boston: Twayne, 1987), p. 200.

17. A summary of Wilson's liberal-democratic goals can be found in Arthur S. Link, *Woodrow Wilson: Revolution, War, and Peace* (Arlington Heights, Ill.: Harlan Davidson, 1979), chapters 1, 4; Ray S. Baker and William E. Dodd, eds., *Woodrow Wilson: Life and Letters* (8 vols., New York: Greenwood Press, 1927–39 [Repr. Westport, Conn., Greenwood Press, 1968]), vol. 7, pp. 180–81; Charles Seymour, ed., *The Intimate Papers of Colonel House* (4 vols., Boston: Houghton Mifflin, 1926–28), vol. 3, p. 38; Thomas Bailey, *Woodrow Wilson and the Lost Peace* (New York: Macmillan, 1944 [Repr. Chicago: Quadrangle Paperbacks, 1963]), pp. 20–22; Jan Willem Schulte-Nordholt, *Woodrow Wilson: A Life for World Peace* (Berkeley: University of California Press, 1991), pp. 237–38; Smith, *Great Departure*, p. 86; and Ambrosius, *Wilsonian Statecraft*, p. 104. As an example of Wilson's attempt to change the Allied war aims at the Paris Peace Conference, see his memorandum to Italian Prime Minister Vittorio E. Orlando of 13 January 1919, *PWW*, vol. 54, pp. 50–51.

18. Wilson conversation with Crosby, 5 July 1918, Baker, *Wilson: Life and Letters*, vol. 8, p. 253; Arno Mayer, *Wilson vs. Lenin: Political Origins of the New Diplomacy, 1917–1918* (Cleveland: Meridian, 1964), p. 170.

19. Until February 1918, the Julian calendar was in effect in Russia. In the twentieth century, it differed by thirteen days from the Gregorian calendar in use in the West. Dates relating to events in Russia prior to 1 (14) February 1918 are given in both the Julian and, following in parentheses, the Gregorian Calendar.

20. Richard Pipes, *The Russian Revolution* (New York: Knopf, 1990), pp. 212–13; W. Bruce Lincoln, *Passage Through Armageddon: The Russians in War and Revolution, 1914–1918* (New York: Simon and Schuster, 1986), pp. 60–61, 88–90; Tsuyoshi Hasegawa, *The February Revolution: Petrograd, 1917* (Seattle: University of Washington Press, 1981), pp. 3, 20–23; Robert Daniels, *Red October: The Bolshevik Revolution of 1917* (Boston: Beacon Press, 1984), p. 9.

21. Martin McCauley, ed., *The Russian Revolution and the Soviet State 1917–1921, Documents* (London: Macmillan, 1975), pp. 8–9; Michael T. Florinsky, *The End of the Russian Empire* (New York: Howard Fertig, 1973), pp. 27–28; Pipes, *Russian Revolution*, p. 272; 1 pud equaled roughly 32 pounds.

22. Hasegawa, *February Revolution*, pp. 91–92.

23. Petrograd became the official Russian name of the city of St. Petersburg after the outbreak of the war with Germany; see Hasegawa, *February Revolution*, p. 4. Observers put the number of demonstrators at between 80,000 and 300,000; see Pipes, *Russian Revolution*, pp. 274–75.

24. J. N. Westwood, *Endurance and Endeavor: Russian History 1812–1992* (New York: Oxford University Press, 1993), pp. 227–28; Lincoln, *Passage Through Armageddon*, p. 322; Daniels, *Red October*, p. 4; Pipes, *Russian Revolution*, p. 281.

25. Robert P. Browder and Alexander F. Kerensky, eds., *The Russian Provisional Government 1917: Documents (RPG)* (3 vols., Stanford, Calif.: Stanford University Press, 1961), vol. 1, p. 23. The Duma had been created after the abortive revolution in 1905 when Tsar Nicholas II agreed to limited political reforms. Political power in Russia, however, had remained centralized in the hands of the Romanov dynasty.

26. Hasegawa, *February Revolution*, p. 354; Vasily V. Shul'gin, *Days of the Russian Revolution: Memoirs from the Right, 1905–1917*, trans. and ed. Bruce F. Adams (Gulf Breeze, Fla.: Academic International Press, 1990), pp. xi–xx; Pipes, *Russian Revolution*, p. 289.

27. *RPG*, vol. 1, p. 78; *Izvestiya*, 2 February (13 March) 1917; McCauley, *Russian Revolution*, pp. 16–18; Hasegawa, *February Revolution*, p. 380.

28. E. N. Burdzhalov, *Russia's Second Revolution: The February 1917 Uprising in Petrograd* (Bloomington: Indiana University Press, 1987), pp. 266–82; Hasegawa, *February Revolution*, pp. 410–11.

29. *RPG*, vol. 2, p. 848; vol. 3, pp. 1210–11; Günther Stökl, *Russische Geschichte* (Stuttgart: Kröner, 1983), p. 638; David Lane, *Politics and Society in the USSR* (New York: New York University Press, 1987), p. 51.

30. Pipes, *Russian Revolution*, pp. 300–1; Reinhard Wittram, *Studien zum Selbstverständnis des 1. und 2. Kabinetts der russischen Provisorischen Regierung, März bis Juli 1917* (Göttingen: Vandenhoek und Ruprecht, 1971), pp. 22, 34; Hasegawa, *February Revolution*, pp. 526–27; Leonard Shapiro, *1917: The Russian Revolution and the Origins of Present-Day Communism* (Hounslow: Maurice Temple Smith, 1984), pp. 64–68; Daniels, *Red October*, p. 13.

31. Miliukov to foreign ambassadors in Petrograd, 4 (17) March 1917, *RPG*, vol. 2, pp. 1042–43; Westwood, *Endurance and Endeavor*, p. 231.

32. Appeal of the Petrograd Soviet, 14 March 1917, *RPG*, vol. 2, pp. 1077–78; War Aims Resolution of the All-Russian Conference of Soviets, *Izvestiya*, 31 March 1917, *RPG*, vol. 2, pp. 1083–84; McCauley, *Russian Revolution*, pp. 24–26; Mayer, *Wilson vs. Lenin*, pp. 67, 73.

33. Press Interview with Miliukov, *Rech'*, 23 March 1917, p. 2, *RPG*, vol. 2, pp. 1044–45.

34. *RPG*, vol. 2, p. 1098; Vladimir Il'ich Lenin, *Collected Works* (45 vols., Moscow: Foreign Language Publishing House, 1960–70), vol. 20, p. 234.

35. *RPG*, vol. 3, pp. 1276–77; Mayer, *Wilson vs. Lenin*, pp. 82–83.

36. David R. Francis, *Russia from the American Embassy, April 1916–November 1918* (New York: Charles Scribner's Sons, 1921), pp. v, 10; George F. Kennan, *Russia Leaves the War* (New York: W.W. Norton, 1984), pp. 35–36.

37. Francis to Lansing, 14 August 1916, Francis, *Russia from the American Embassy*, p. 23; Francis to Lansing, 23 February 1917, Jamie H. Cockfield, ed., *Dollars and Diplomacy: Ambassador David Rowland Francis and the Fall of Tsarism, 1916–1917* (Durham, N.C.: Duke University Press, 1981), p. 85.

38. As quoted in Cockfield, *Dollars and Diplomacy*, p. 91.

39. *FRUS*, 1918, Russia (3 vols., Washington, D.C.: GPO, 1931–32), vol. 1, pp. 5–6.

40. Ibid., p. 6.

41. Ibid., p. 12.

42. *PWW*, vol. 41, p. 524.

43. George F. Kennan, *Russia and the West Under Lenin and Stalin* (New York: Mentor, 1961), p. 24.

44. As quoted in David F. Houston, *Eight Years with Wilson's Cabinet, 1913 to 1920*, 2 vols. (Garden City, N.Y.: Doubleday, 1926), vol. 1, p. 245; *PWW*, vol. 42, p. 37.

45. *FRUS*, 1918, Russia, vol. 1, pp. 18–20, 21–24.

46. John Lewis Gaddis, *Russia, the Soviet Union, and the United States: An Interpretive History* (New York: John Wiley and Sons, 1978), p. 65.

47. *PWW*, vol. 42, pp. 36–37.

48. The Imperial German government did indeed pay several million marks to the Bolsheviks prior to the October Revolution. In his edition of documents from the Archives of the German foreign ministry, Z.A.B. Zeman concluded that there was "no evidence among the documents of the Foreign Ministry that Lenin . . . was in direct contact with any of the official German agencies. How much he knew about the activities of the men around him is difficult to tell." See Z.A.B. Zeman, ed., *Germany and the Revolution in Russia, 1915–1918: Documents from the Archives of the German Foreign Ministry* (London: Oxford University Press, 1958), pp. x–xi. In an effort to provide proof about a German-Bolshevik conspiracy, Edgar Sisson of the Committee on Public Information received documents, later called the "Sisson Documents," that allegedly proved such a conspiracy. The documents, however, were forgeries. See *FRUS*, 1918, Russia, vol. 1, pp. 372–78; Memorandum by Secretary of State Robert Lansing, 4 December 1917, *PWW*, vol. 45, pp. 205–7; Root to Lansing, 27

August 1917, *FRUS*, 1918, Russia, vol. 1, p. 139; Lansing to Wilson, 10 December 1917, *PWW*, vol. 45, pp. 263–65; *RPG*, vol. 3, pp. 1364–81. American representatives in Russia also reported in November and December 1917 that the Bolsheviks were working with Russian Monarchists; see Francis to Lansing, 10 December 1917, *FRUS*, 1918, Russia, vol. 1, p. 296.

49. U.S. Department of State, Records Relating to the Internal Affairs of Russia and the Soviet Union, 1918–29, Record Group 59, Decimal File 861.00/423 1/2 A, National Archives, Washington, D.C; *PWW*, vol. 42, p. 463.

50. Miliukov's note, *RPG*, vol. 2, p. 1098; Wilson to the Provisional Government, 22 May 1917, *PWW*, vol. 42, pp. 365–67.

51. U.S. Department of State, Record Group 59, Decimal File 861.00/361, N.A.; *PWW*, vol. 42, p. 318.

52. *PWW*, vol. 42, p. 367.

53. Ibid., pp. 36, 44.

54. *FRUS*, 1918, Russia, vol. 1, p. 109; Philip C. Jessup, *Elihu Root* (2 vols., New York: Dodd, Mead, and Co., 1938), vol. 2, p. 356; *PWW*, vol. 42, p. 262.

55. As quoted in Jessup, *Root*, vol. 2, p. 356.

56. *PWW*, vol. 42, p. 194.

57. Jessup, *Root*, vol. 2, p. 357.

58. Paraphrase of undated telegram, received American Embassy, Petrograd, 30 June [1917], Box 7, p. 1155, Charles Edward Russell Papers, Library of Congress (L.C.), Washington, D.C.

59. Lansing to Francis, 22 May 1917, *FRUS*, 1918, Russia, vol. 1, p. 111.

60. Summers to Lansing, 27 June 1917 , *FRUS*, 1918, Russia, vol. 1, pp. 125–27; Jessup, *Root*, vol. 2, p. 363.

61. Root to Lansing, 17 June 1917, *FRUS*, 1918, Russia, vol. 1, pp. 121–22; Root to McAdoo, 2 July 1917, *FRUS*, 1918, Russia, vol. 1, p. 128.

62. Polk to Francis, 7 July, *FRUS*, 1918, Russia, vol. 1, p. 129; Jessup, *Root*, vol. 2, pp. 364–66.

63. Root to Lansing [August 1917], *FRUS*, 1918, Russia, vol. 1, p. 140; Jessup, *Root*, vol. 2, p. 367.

64. Root to Lansing [August 1917], *FRUS*, 1918, Russia, vol. 1, p. 144.

65. Supplementary Report of the Special Diplomatic Mission to Russia to Lansing [August 1917], *FRUS*, 1918, Russia, vol. 1, pp. 147–53; Jessup, *Root*, p. 364.

66. Kennan, *Russia Leaves the War*, p. 50; David W. McFadden, *Alternative Path: Soviets and Americans, 1917–1920* (New York: Oxford University Press, 1993), p. 87.

67. As quoted in Jessup, *Root*, vol. 2, p. 369.

68. Jessup, *Root*, vol. 2, pp. 367–68.

69. *FRUS*, 1918, Russia, vol. 3, pp. 9, 10, 4, 25; *RPG*, vol. 2, p. 502.

70. *FRUS*, 1918 Russia, vol. 3, p. 12; Francis, *Russia from the American Embassy*, p. 124.

71. *RPG*, vol. 2, p. 925.

72. Ibid., p. 928.

73. Ibid., pp. 942, 937.

74. *RPG*, vol. 1, p. 4; Mayer, *Wilson vs. Lenin*, p. 250.

75. *RPG*, vol. 2, p. 967.

76. Kennan, *Russia and the West Under Lenin and Stalin*, p. 36.

77. Robert F. Lansing, "Memorandum on Russian Situation and the Root Mission, 9 August 1917," as quoted in William A. Williams, *American-Russian Relations, 1781–1947* (New York: Holt, Rinehart and Co., 1952), p. 95.

78. Baker, *Wilson: Life and Letters*, vol. 6, p. 320.

79. Russell to Wilson, 7 November 1917, *PWW*, vol. 44, p. 558; Wilson to Russell, 10 November, ibid.

80. Wilson to Clark, 13 November 1917, *PWW*, vol. 45, p. 39.

CHAPTER 2

1. Ray S. Baker and William E. Dodd, eds., *Woodrow Wilson: Life and Letters* (8 vols., New York: Greenwood Press, 1927–39 [Repr. Westport, Conn., Greenwood Press, 1968]), vol. 8, p. 95.

2. Woodrow Wilson to Lindley M. Garrison, 8 August 1914, Arthur S. Link, ed., *The Papers of Woodrow Wilson (PWW)* (68 vols., Princeton, N.J.: Princeton University Press, 1966–93), vol. 30, p. 262; Wilson to Frank Clark, 13 November 1917, *PWW*, vol. 45, p. 39.

3. Roland N. Stromberg, *European Intellectual History Since 1789* (4th ed., Englewood Cliffs, N.J.: Prentice-Hall, 1986), p. 16; Wilson as quoted in Richard Hofstadter, *American Political Tradition and the Men Who Made It* (New York: Knopf, 1973), pp. 242–43.

4. Woodrow Wilson, "Edmund Burke," Address, 31 August 1893, *PWW*, vol. 8, p. 341.

5. Robert H. Ferrell, *Woodrow Wilson and World War I, 1917–1921* (New York: Harper and Row, 1985), pp. 52–53.

6. Zimmermann memorandum, 27 November 1914, as quoted in Z.A.B. Zeman, ed., *Germany and the Revolution in Russia, 1915–1918: Documents from the Archives of the German Foreign Ministry* (London: Oxford University Press, 1958), pp. vii–xi.

7. Romberg to Bethmann-Hollweg, 30 September 1915, Zeman, *Germany and the Revolution in Russia*, p. 6; Brockdorff-Rantzau to Zimmermann, 2 April 1917, ibid., p. 31; Hauptmann Hülsen, German General

Staff, to Foreign Ministry, 30 March 1917, ibid., pp. 27–28; Busche to Romberg, 4 April 1917, ibid., p. 34; Robert P. Browder and Alexander F. Kerensky, eds., *The Russian Provisional Government 1917: Documents (RPG)* (3 vols., Stanford, Calif.: Stanford University Press, 1961), vol. 2, pp. 1090–96; W. Bruce Lincoln, *Passage Through Armageddon: The Russians in War and Revolution, 1914–1918* (New York: Simon and Schuster, 1986), p. 363.

8. Richard Pipes, *The Russian Revolution* (New York: Knopf, 1990), pp. 345–48; Leonard Shapiro, *1917: The Russian Revolution and the Origins of Present-Day Communism* (Hounslow: Maurice Temple Smith, 1984), p. 28; Vladimir I. Lenin, "First Letter from Afar," 7 (20) March 1917, *Pravda*, 21, 22 March; Lenin, *Collected Works* (45 vols., Moscow: Foreign Language Publishing House, 1960–70), vol. 23, p. 299; Lenin, "First Letter from Afar," *Collected Works*, vol. 23, p. 300; "Fourth Letter from Afar," *Collected Works*, vol. 23, pp. 337–38.

9. Lenin, *Collected Works*, vol. 23, p. 338; Robert Service, "The Bolsheviks on Political Campaign in 1917: A Case Study of the War Question," in Edith Ragovin Frankel et al., eds., *Revolution in Russia: Reassessments of 1917* (New York: Cambridge University Press, 1992), pp. 307–10.

10. Kühlmann memorandum, 3 December 1917, Zeman, *Germany and the Revolution in Russia*, p. 94; *RPG*, vol. 3, p. 1381; Arno J. Mayer, *Wilson vs. Lenin: Political Origins of the New Diplomacy, 1917–1918* (Cleveland: Meridian, 1964), p. 67.

11. Pipes, *Russian Revolution*, pp. 574–75.

12. *RPG*, vol. 3, p. 1206.

13. *FRUS*, 1918, Russia (3 vols., Washington, D.C.: GPO, 1931–32), vol. 1, p. 34.

14. Ibid., p. 50.

15. Martin McCauley, ed., *The Russian Revolution and the Soviet State 1917–1921, Documents* (London: Macmillan, 1975), p. 113. Emphasis in original.

16. David R. Francis, *Russia from the American Embassy, April 1916–November 1918* (New York: Charles Scribner's Sons, 1921), pp. 180–81; Robert Daniels, *Red October: The Bolshevik Revolution of 1917* (Boston: Beacon Press, 1984), p. 197. Prime Minister Kerensky, however, eluded the Soviets. He had left the palace hours before to gather pro-government support among front troops.

17. Isaac Deutscher, *The Prophet Armed: Trotsky 1879–1921* (New York: Oxford University Press, 1954), pp. 325–27.

18. Karl-Heinz Ruffmann, *Sowjetrussland* (München: Deutscher Taschenbuch Verlag, 1981), p. 32; Adam Ulam, *Expansion and Coexistence: Soviet Foreign Policy 1917–1933* (2d ed., New York: Holt, Rinehart

and Winston, 1974), p. 40; Gottfried Schramm, "Die Endkrise des Zarismus, allgemeines oder partielles Versagen?" in Manfred Hellmann et al., eds., *Handbuch der Geschichte Russlands* (3 vols., Stuttgart: Hiersemann, 1976-89), vol. 3, p. 619; Dietrich Geyer, *The Russian Revolution* (New York: St. Martin's Press, 1987), pp. 116-17.

19. Jane Degras, ed., *Soviet Documents on Foreign Policy* (3 vols., New York: Oxford University Press, 1951 [Repr. New York:Octagon, 1978]), vol. 1, p. 1.

20. Ibid., p. 6. The treaties were subsequently published in Great Britain and the United States.

21. Jan Willem Schulte-Nordholt, *Woodrow Wilson: A Life for World Peace* (Berkeley: University of California Press, 1991), p. 243.

22. Degras, *Documents*, vol. 1, p. 4; Francis to Lansing, 27 November 1917, *FRUS*, 1918, Russia, vol. 1, p. 250.

23. George F. Kennan. *Russia Leaves the War* (New York: W. W. Norton, 1984), pp. 75-76; Richard K. Debo, *Revolution and Survival: The Foreign Policy of Soviet Russia, 1917-1918* (Toronto: University of Toronto Press, 1979), p. 17. The publication of the secret Allied war-aims treaties of the years 1915 through 1917 in the newspaper *Izvestiya* on 22 November 1917, and in Western newspapers, such as the *New York Times* on 25 November and the *Manchester Guardian* on 13 December, served the same purpose. In those treaties, the British, French, Russian, and Italian governments had agreed upon postwar national boundaries and spheres of influence. The agreements, Trotsky alleged, were designed by the imperialist countries to leave their populations ignorant of their true interests. The people of Europe, he continued, had a right to learn for which aims they were fighting. Degras, *Soviet Documents*, vol. 1, pp. 8-9; Ray S. Baker, ed., *Woodrow Wilson and World Settlement: Written from His Unpublished Personal Materials* (3 vols., Garden City, N.Y.: Doubleday, 1922), vol. 1, pp. 47-63.

24. Francis to Lansing, 28 November 1917, *FRUS*, 1918, Russia, vol. 1, pp. 251-52; Degras, *Documents*, vol. 1, p. 19.

25. *Washington Post*, 9 November 1917.

26. *FRUS* 1918, Russia, vol. 1, pp. 291, 325. Brackets in original.

27. The *New York Times* reported on 17 November that the State Department had complained the day before about being "unable to understand what was happening in Russia." "Kerensky" in Joseph L. Wieczynski, ed., *Modern Encyclopedia of Russian and Soviet History* (46 vols., Gulf Breeze, Fla.: Academic International Press, 1976-87), vol. 16, p. 111.

28. Bullitt to Wilson, 7 December 1917, *PWW*, vol. 45, p. 235; Ronald Steel, *Walter Lippmann and the American Century* (New York: Vintage, 1980), p. 137.

29. Diary of Josephus Daniels, November 27, 1917, as quoted in *PWW*, vol. 45, p. 147. Abbreviations in the original.

30. Wilson Address before Labor Convention in Buffalo, 12 November 1917, *PWW*, vol. 45, p. 14.

31. Kennan. *Russia Leaves the War*, p. 244; August Heckscher, *Woodrow Wilson* (New York: Charles Scribner's, 1991), pp. 47–72.

32. *FRUS*, 1919, Paris Peace Conference (13 vols., Washington, D.C.: GPO, 1942–47), vol. 1, pp. 45–46.

33. Charles Seymour, ed., *The Intimate Papers of Colonel House* (4 vols. Boston: Houghton Mifflin, 1928), vol. 3, *Into the War*, p. 282.

34. Charles Seymour, *American Diplomacy During the World War* (Baltimore: Johns Hopkins University Press, 1934 [Repr. Westport, Conn.: Greenwood Press, 1975]), p. 281; Seymour, *Papers of Colonel House*, vol. 3, pp. 284–85.

35. House Diary, 2, 3 December 1917, as quoted in Seymour, *American Diplomacy*, p. 283.

36. Seymour, *Papers of Colonel House*, vol. 3, p. 41.

37. Wilson, State of the Union Message Before Congress, 4 December 1917, *PWW*, vol. 45, p. 199.

38. *PWW*, vol. 45, p. 199.

39. As quoted in Linda Killen, "The Search for a Democratic Russia: The Wilson Administration's Russian Policy, 1917–1921" (Ph.D. diss., University of North Carolina, 1975), p. 51; *FRUS*, The Lansing Papers, 1914–20 (2 vols., Washington, D.C.: GPO, 1940), vol. 2, p. 343; Lansing to Wilson, 2 January 1918, *PWW*, vol. 45, pp. 427–28.

40. Robert Lansing, *War Memoirs of Robert Lansing, Secretary of State* (New York: Bobbs-Merrill, 1935), p. 241.

41. Spring-Rice to Balfour, 4 January 1918, *PWW*, vol. 45, p. 456.

42. *PWW*, vol. 45, pp. 456–57.

43. *FRUS*, 1918, Russia, vol. 1, pp. 405, 422–24; Edgar Sisson, *25 November–4 March 1918: One Hundred Red Days. A Personal Chronicle of the Bolshevik Revolution.* (New Haven, Conn.: Yale University Press, 1931), p. 205.

44. *FRUS*, 1918, Russia, vol. 2, p. vii; Kennan. *Russia Leaves the War*, p. 257.

45. Wilson, Address Before Joint Session of Congress, 8 January 1918, *PWW*, vol. 45, pp. 534–35.

46. Kennan, *Russia Leaves the War*, pp. 254–55.

47. *Washington Post*, 5 January 1918.

48. *PWW*, vol. 45, p. 537.

49. *Pravda*, 2 November 1917, as quoted in Manfred Hellmann, ed., *Die russische Revolution. Von der Abdankung des Zaren bis zum Staatsstreich der Bolschewiki* (5th ed., München: Deutscher Taschenbuch Verlag, 1984), pp. 338–39.

50. Claude E. Fike, "The United States and Russian Territorial Problems, 1917–1920," *The Historian* 24 (1962), p. 335; Betty M. Unterberger, "National Self-Determination," in Alexandre De Conde, ed., *Encyclopedia of American Foreign Policy* (3 vols., New York: Scribner's 1978), vol. 2, p. 640.

51. Seymour, *Intimate Papers of Colonel House*, vol. 3, p. 331.

52. Sisson, *25 November 1917–4 March 1918: One Hundred Red Days*, p. 209; McFadden, *Alternative Paths*, p. 102; John M. Thompson, *Russia, Bolshevism, and the Versailles Peace* (Princeton, N.J.: Princeton University Press, 1966), p. 18.

53. Francis to Lansing, 22 November 1917, *FRUS*, 1918, Russia, vol. 1, p. 244; Francis to Lansing, 22 November 1917, *FRUS*, 1918, Russia, vol. 1, p. 245; Francis to Lansing, 27 November 1917, *FRUS*, 1918, Russia, vol. 1, p. 250; Francis to Lansing, 28 November 1917, *FRUS*, 1918, Russia, vol. 1, pp. 251–52.

54. Degras, *Soviet Documents on Foreign Policy*, vol. 1, pp. 21–22. Those conditions were known in the State Department; see Morris to Lansing, 27 December 1917, *FRUS*, 1918, Russia, vol. 1, p. 404.

55. Service, "The Bolsheviks on Political Campaign," p. 306.

56. Degras, *Soviet Documents on Foreign Policy*, vol. 1, pp. 40–41; Deutscher, *Trotsky*, pp. 373–75.

57. Department of State, *Proceedings of the Brest-Litovsk Conference*, Minutes of 10 February 1918 (Washington, D.C.: GPO, 1918), p. 172; Deutscher, *Trotsky*, p. 394.

58. Debo, *Revolution and Survival*, p. 171; Deutscher, *Trotsky*, p. 355.

59. *PWW*, vol. 46, p. 341; Ruggles to General Headquarters, Supreme War Council, 27 February 1918, Box 321, Tasker H. Bliss Papers.

60. *FRUS*, 1918 Russia, vol. 1, p. 337; *PWW*, vol. 46. p. 45.

61. Francis to Lansing, 12 March 1918, *FRUS*, 1918, Russia, vol. 1, pp. 398, 392.

62. *FRUS*, 1918, Russia, vol. 1, pp. 395–96.

63. Debo, *Revolution and Survival*, p. 174.

CHAPTER 3

1. As quoted in George F. Kennan, *The Decision to Intervene* (New York: W. W. Norton, 1984), p. 405.

2. Richard K. Debo, *Revolution and Survival: The Foreign Policy of Soviet Russia, 1917–1918* (Toronto: University of Toronto Press, 1979), p. 231.

3. Summers to Lansing, 27 November 1917, Department of State, *Papers Relating to the Foreign Relations of the United States (FRUS)*, 1918, Russia (3 vols., Washington, D.C.: GPO, 1931–32), vol. 1, pp. 270–71,

254; Robert F. Lansing, *War Memoirs of Robert Lansing* (New York: Bobbs-Merrill, 1935), p. 345.

4. Caroline K. Cumming and Walter W. Pettit, eds., *Russian-American Relations, March 1917–March 1920: Documents and Papers* (New York: Harcourt, 1920 [Repr. Westport, Conn., Hyperion Press]), p. 94; *FRUS*, 1918, Russia, vol. 1, p. 316.

5. *FRUS*, 1918, Russia, vol. 1, p. 356; David W. McFadden, *Alternative Path: Soviets and Americans, 1917–1920* (New York: Oxford University Press, 1993), p. 80.

6. Jane Degras, ed., *Soviet Documents on Foreign Policy* (3 vols., New York: Oxford University Press, 1951 [Repr. New York: Octagon, 1978]), vol. 1, pp. 14–15.

7. *Izvestiya*, November 20, 1917; English translation printed in Degras, ed., *Soviet Documents on Foreign Policy*, vol. 1, pp. 14–15; Francis to Lansing, 2 December 1917, *FRUS*, 1918, Russia, vol. 1, p. 282; Francis to Lansing, 1 December 1917, *FRUS*, 1918, Russia, vol. 1, p. 279; Judson to War Department, 1 December 1917, *FRUS*, 1918, Russia, vol. 1, p. 279; Lansing to Francis, 6 December 1917, *FRUS*, 1918, Russia, vol. 1, p. 289; McFadden, *Alternative Path*, pp. 60–61.

8. *FRUS*, The Lansing Papers, 1914–20 (2 vols., Washington, D.C.: GPO, 1940), vol. 2, p. 346.

9. Manfred Hellmann, ed., *Die russische Revolution: Von der Abdankung des Zaren bis zum Staatsstreich der Bolschewiki* (5th ed., München: Deutscher Taschenbuch Verlag, 1984), p. 272.

10. *FRUS*, Lansing Papers, vol. 2, p. 345n. 28; George F. Kennan, *Russia Leaves the War* (New York: W. W. Norton, 1984), p. 181.

11. *FRUS*, 1918, Russia, vol. 2, p. 612; Kennan, *Russia Leaves the War*, p. 183.

12. *FRUS*, 1918, Russia, vol. 2, p. 21.

13. Arthur S. Link, ed., *The Papers of Woodrow Wilson (PWW)* (68 vols., Princeton, N.J.: Princeton University Press, 1966–93), vol. 45, p. 420; John Silverlight, *The Victors' Dilemma: Allied Intervention in the Russian Civil War* (New York: Weybright and Talley, 1971), pp. 16–17.

14. *FRUS*, 1918, Russia, vol. 2, p. 29.

15. Ibid., p. 49.

16. Ray S. Baker and William E. Dodd, eds., *Woodrow Wilson: Life and Letters* (New York: Greenwood Press, 1927–39 [Repr. Westport, Conn: Greenwood Press, 1968]), vol. 8, pp. 1–2.

17. Ibid., p. 2.

18. Charles F. Seymour, ed., *The Intimate Papers of Colonel House* (4 vols., Boston: Houghton Mifflin, 1926–28), vol. 3, pp. 393–94.

19. *FRUS*, 1918, Russia, vol. 2, p. 67; Baker, *Wilson: Life and Letters*, vol. 8, pp. 8, 12.

20. *PWW*, vol. 46, p. 571.

21. Ibid., vol. 47, p. 62.

22. Ibid., pp. 80–81.

23. Ibid., pp. 69–71.

24. Ibid., p. 68.

25. Ibid., pp. 140–41.

26. Ibid., pp. 319–20.

27. *FRUS*, 1918, Russia, vol. 2, p. 119.

28. *PWW*, vol. 47, p. 357. Italics in original.

29. "Movements for Autonomy in Siberia," April 22, 1918, *PWW*, vol. 47, pp. 397–99; "The Military Advance of Semenoff," May 22, 1918, *PWW*, vol. 48, pp. 104–106.

30. For estimates of the number of Czechs fighting on the Allied side, see James Bunyan, ed., *Intervention, Civil War, and Communism in Russia, April–December 1918: Documents and Materials* (Baltimore: Johns Hopkins University Press, 1936 [Repr. New York: Octagon Books, 1976]), pp. 75, 77. Miles's much higher estimates of the number of Czech troops were based on the limited information about the Siberian situation available to him. The highest estimation of Czech troops can be found in an article by the German journalist Hans Vorst, which was reprinted in the *New Republic* on 5 October 1918 (p. 288). Vorst estimated the number of Czech troops to be as high as 300,000; see Kennan, *Decision to Intervene*, pp. 138–39.

31. Bunyan, *Intervention, Civil War and Communism*, pp. 77, 80–83, 87.

32. *FRUS*, 1918, Russia, vol. 2, p. 226–27, 189, 246; *PWW*, vol. 48, p. 398. In this memorandum, Lansing estimated that there were between 50,000 and 75,000 Czech soldiers.

33. Wilson and Wiseman, as quoted in N. Gordon Levin, *Woodrow Wilson and World Politics: America's Response to War and Revolution* (New York: Oxford University Press, 1968), p. 96.

34. *FRUS*, 1918, Russia, vol. 2, pp. 262–63.

35. *PWW*, vol. 48, pp. 640–42.

36. Memorandum, "Notes of Conversation with Mr. C. T. Williams, deputy commissioner, American Red Cross Mission to Russia," 22 February 1919, p. 1, Box 357, Bliss Papers; Benjamin D. Rhodes, *The Anglo-American Winter War with Russia, 1918–1919: A Diplomatic and Military Tragicomedy* (New York: Greenwood, 1988), p. ix and Chapter 3, "The Americans Arrive."

37. House diary, 19 September 1918, as quoted in John M. Thompson, *Russia, Bolshevism, and the Versailles Peace* (Princeton, N.J.: Princeton University Press, 1966), p. 45.

38. "How Not to Help Russia," *The Nation* 106 (1 June 1918), pp. 639–40; Villard as quoted in Thomas Knock, *To End All Wars: Woodrow Wilson and the Quest for a New World Order* (New York: Oxford University Press, 1992), p. 157.

39. William S. Graves, *America's Siberian Adventure, 1918–1920* (New York: J. Cape and Harrison, 1931), pp. 4, 55.

40. Ibid., pp. 67, 341, 217; *FRUS*, 1918, Russia, vol. 2, p. 417.

41. Robert Lansing. "Memorandum on Absolutism and Bolshevism," 26 October 1918, as quoted in Ephraim K. Smith, "Robert Lansing and the Paris Peace Conference" (Ph.D. diss., Johns Hopkins University 1972), pp. 109–10.

42. *PWW*, vol. 53, pp. 227–29.

43. *PWW*, vol. 51, p. 350, vol. 53, p. 221; Betty M. Unterberger, "Woodrow Wilson and the Bolsheviks. The 'Acid Test' of Soviet-American Relations," *Diplomatic History* 11 (1987), p. 85.

44. Rhodes, *Anglo-American Winter War*, p. 20; Kennan, *The Decision to Intervene*, p. 403; N.Gordon Levin. "American Intervention: Aid to Liberal Russia," in Betty M. Unterberger, ed., *American Intervention in the Russian Civil War* (Lexington, Mass.: Heath, 1969), p. 93; Levin, *Woodrow Wilson and World Politics*, p. 102; William A. Williams. "American Intervention: Strictly Anti-Bolshevik," in Unterberger, *American Intervention in the Russian Civil War*, p. 93.

45. Kennan, *The Decision to Intervene*, pp. 348–50.

46. The Czechoslovaks did not need American help to leave Russia. Secretary of War Baker noted on February 19, 1920: "The number of our troops remaining in Siberia is something like 5,000 and it is obvious that their assistance is not necessary to some 72,000 Czecho-Slovaks. . . . If the small detachments of Americans . . . had difficulty in getting out, they could be protected by the Czecho-Slovaks" *(FRUS*, 1920 [3 vols., Washington, D.C.: GPO, 1936], vol. 3, p. 503). Eugene P. Trani, "Woodrow Wilson and the Decision to Intervene in Russia: A Reconsideration," *Journal of Modern History* 48 (1976): pp. 445–47; *PWW*, vol. 49, pp. 67–68, abbreviations in the original; Baker to Ralph Hayes, 24 December 1929, as quoted in Baker, *Wilson: Life and Letters*, vol. 8, p. 284n. 1.

47. Levin, *Woodrow Wilson and World Politics*, p. 101; Thompson, *Russia, Bolshevism, and the Versailles Peace*, p. 34.

CHAPTER 4

1. Winston S. Churchill, *The Aftermath: The World Crisis, 1918–1928* (New York: Charles Scribner's Sons, 1929), pp. 243–44.

2. John M. Thompson, *Russia, Bolshevism, and the Versailles Peace* (Princeton, N.J.: Princeton University Press, 1966), Chapter 3; Secretary

of War Baker, Memorandum to Wilson, 27 November 1918, *PWW*, vol. 53, pp. 227–29.

3. Prime Ministers Clemenceau and Lloyd George argued that only leaders of governments but no heads of state should be represented at the conference.

4. Robert F. Lansing, *The Big Four and Others of the Peace Conference* (Boston: Houghton Mifflin, 1921), pp. 38–39; Cobb Memorandum to House, 4 November 1918, Arthur S. Link, ed., *The Papers of Woodrow Wilson (PWW)* (68 vols., Princeton, N.J.: Princeton University Press, 1966–93), vol. 51, pp. 590–91; Herbert C. Hoover, *The Ordeal of Woodrow Wilson* (New York: McGraw-Hill, 1958), pp. 61, 64–66; Jan Willem Schulte-Nordholt, *Woodrow Wilson: A Life for World Peace* (Berkeley: University of California Press, 1991), p. 282. For an analysis of the arguments for and against Wilson's attending the conference, see Thomas A. Bailey, *Woodrow Wilson and the Lost Peace* (New York: Macmillan, 1944 [Repr. Chicago: Quadrangle Paperbacks, 1963]), pp. 73–86.

5. David Lloyd George, *Memoirs of the Peace Conference* (2 vols., New Haven, Conn.: Yale University Press, 1939), vol. 1, pp. 140–41; Harold Nicolson, *Peacemaking 1919* (New York: Grosset and Dunlap, 1965), pp. 198–99; Schulte-Nordholt, *Wilson*, pp. 288–91; Robert H. Ferrell, *Woodrow Wilson and World War I, 1917–1921* (New York: Harper and Row, 1985), p. 152.

6. Notes of Conversation, 12 January 1919, Department of State, *Papers Relating to the Foreign Relations of the United States (FRUS)*, 1919, Russia (Washington, D.C.: GPO, 1937), p. 5. Four days later, on 16 January, Lloyd George "clarified" that he did not want to offer the Soviets diplomatic recognition. His goal was merely to get various Russian groups, including the Bolsheviks, to Paris for negotiations. Notes of Conversation, 16 January, 10:30 A.M., *FRUS*, 1919, Russia, p. 11.

7. Lloyd George, *Memoirs of the Peace Conference*, pp. 207–10, 218–19; *FRUS*, 1919, Russia, pp. 2–3; *FRUS*, The Paris Peace Conference (13 vols., Washington, D.C.: GPO, 1942–47), vol. 3, pp. 650–51; *PWW*, vol. 54, pp. 53–54.

8. Barclay to Polk, 13 January 1919, *FRUS*, 1919, Russia, p. 7; Notes of Conversation, 21 January, *FRUS*, 1919, Russia, p. 21; John Silverlight, *The Victors' Dilemma: Allied Intervention in the Russian Civil War* (New York: Weybright and Talley, 1971), p. 141; August Heckscher, *Woodrow Wilson* (New York: Charles Scribner's Sons, 1991), p. 516.

9. *FRUS*, Paris Peace Conference, vol. 1, pp. 266–71.

10. Thompson, *Russia, Bolshevism, and the Versailles Peace*, p. 47.

11. Litvinov to Wilson, 24 December 1918, Jane Degras, ed., *Soviet Documents on Foreign Policy* (3 vols., New York: Oxford University Press, 1951 [Repr. Octagon, 1978]), vol. 1, p. 131.

12. Degras, *Documents*, vol. 1, p. 132; Thompson, *Russia, Bolshevism, and the Versailles Peace*, p. 90.

13. David R. Francis, *Russia from the American Embassy, April 1916–November 1918* (New York: Charles Scribner's Sons, 1921), pp. 306–10.

14. Tasker H. Bliss, Diary, 7 January 1919, pp. 84–85, Box 244, Tasker S. Bliss Papers, Library of Congress.

15. David W. McFadden, *Alternative Path: Soviets and Americans, 1917–1920* (New York: Oxford University Press, 1993), p. 193.

16. *FRUS*, Paris Peace Conference, vol. 3, pp. 626–27, 639. In his *Memoirs of the Peace Conference*, Lloyd George said that Noulens was "not a good witness." He was a "shallow and unintelligent partisan rather than a witness. He repeated the gossip and hearsay of the Parisian journals of the Extreme Right about the horrors of Bolshevism" (p. 222).

17. *FRUS*, Paris Peace Conference, vol. 3, pp. 643–46; *FRUS*, 1919, Russia, pp. 4, 15–17; Arthur Upham Pope, *Maxim Litvinoff* (New York: L. B. Fischer, 1943), p. 152; McFadden, *Alternative Path*, pp. 182–86.

18. *FRUS*, 1919, Russia, p. 16.

19. *The Bullitt Mission to Russia, Testimony of William C. Bullitt before the Committee on Foreign Relations, United States Senate* (New York: H. W. Huebsch, 1919), pp. 5–6; Notes of Conversation, 21 January, *FRUS*, 1919, Russia, p. 21.

20. *FRUS*, 1919, Russia, p. 21.

21. Ibid.

22. *PWW*, vol. 6, p. 229.

23. *FRUS*, 1919, Russia, p. 31.

24. *FRUS*, Paris Peace Conference, vol. 3, p. 677.

25. Joan Hoff-Wilson, *Ideology and Economics: U.S. Relations with the Soviet Union, 1918–1933* (Columbia: University of Missouri Press, 1974), pp. 32–33; N. Gordon Levin, *Woodrow Wilson and World Politics: America's Response to War and Revolution* (New York: Oxford University Press, 1968), p. 210; Thompson, *Russia, Bolshevism, and the Versailles Peace*, p. 109.

26. Degras, *Documents*, vol. 1, pp. 137–39; Thompson, *Russia, Bolshevism, and the Versailles Peace*, pp. 116–17.

27. Memorandum, Russian Embassy in France to Peace Conference, 12 February 1919, *FRUS*, 1919, Russia, pp. 53–54.

28. Minutes of 14th Session of the Supreme War Council, 14 February 1919, *FRUS*, 1919, Russia, pp. 57–58.

29. Lansing to Polk, 17 February 1919, *FRUS*, 1919, Russia, pp. 68–69; *FRUS*, Paris Peace Conference, vol. 4, pp. 10–13.

30. Wilson to Commission to Negotiate Peace, 19 February 1919, *FRUS*, 1919, Russia, pp. 71–72.

31. *Bullitt Mission*, p. 34; Thompson, *Russia, Bolshevism, and the Versailles Peace*, pp. 147–48.

32. Bullitt to House, 7 February 1918, as quoted in Beatrice Farnsworth, *William C. Bullitt and the Soviet Union* (Bloomington: Indiana University Press, 1967), pp. 15, 17; Thompson, *Russia, Bolshevism, and the Versailles Peace*, p. 161.

33. *Bullitt Mission to Russia*, p. 66; McFadden, *Alternative Path*, pp. 219–20.

34. *Bullitt Mission to Russia*, pp. 34–35.

35. Ibid., pp. 36–37; Buckler Memorandum, 31 January 1919, *FRUS*, 1919, Russia, p. 38. The French government was not informed about Bullitt's mission because of the assumption that it would not approve; see George F. Kennan, *Russia and the West under Lenin and Stalin* (New York: Mentor, 1961), p. 127.

36. Haynes to Commission to Negotiate Peace, 11 March 1919, *FRUS*, 1919, Russia, p. 76.

37. Bullitt to Commission to Negotiate Peace, 16 March 1919, *FRUS*, 1919, Russia, pp. 78–79.

38. *FRUS*, 1919, Russia, p. 80; Bullitt to Commission to Negotiate Peace, 18 March 1919, *FRUS*, 1919, Russia, pp. 81–83.

39. Degras, *Documents*, vol. 1, pp. 147–50; McFadden, *Alternative Path*, p. 231; Mayer, *Politics and Diplomacy of Peacemaking*, pp. 469–70.

40. *Bullitt Mission to Russia*, pp. 65–66.

41. Mayer, *Politics and Diplomacy of Peacemaking*, p. 470; *Bullitt Mission to Russia*, p. 66; Wickham Steed, "The Intrigue That May Be Revised," *Daily Mail*, 27 March 1919. Steed received his information about Bullitt's negotiations with Lenin from Gordon Auchincloss of the American delegation. Historian John M. Thompson believed that the conservative Auchincloss leaked the information because he wanted to derail an agreement with the Soviets. See *Russia, Bolshevism, and the Versailles Peace*, p. 237.

42. *Bullitt Mission to Russia*, p. 73.

43. Ibid., p. 90.

44. Edwin E. Weinstein, *Woodrow Wilson: A Medical and Psychological Biography* (Princeton, N.J.: Princeton University Press, 1981), pp. xv, 323.

45. *FRUS*, 1919, Russia, p. 102; Hoover, *Ordeal of Woodrow Wilson*, p. 120.

46. *Bullitt Mission to Russia*, p. 83; *FRUS*, 1919, Russia, p. 108.

47. Swenson to Commission to Negotiate Peace, 14 May 1919, *FRUS*, 1919, Russia, pp. 112, 114–15.

48. Thompson, *Russia, Bolshevism, and the Versailles Peace*, pp. 259–62.

49. *FRUS*, 1919, Russia, p. 115.

50. Patrick A. Taylor, "Kolchak, Aleksandr Vasil'evich," in Joseph L. Wieczinski, ed., *Modern Encyclopedia of Russian and Soviet History* (46 vols., Gulf Breeze, Fla.: Academic International Press, 1976–87), vol. 17, pp. 12–13; Mayer, *Politics and Diplomacy of Peacemaking*, p. 486; Joshua Roset, "The Rise of a New Russian Autocracy," *The New Republic*, 9 July 1919, pp. 316–24; George Stewart, *The White Armies of Russia: A Chronicle of Counter-Revolution and Allied Intervention* (New York: Macmillan, 1933), chapters X–XII.

51. *FRUS*, 1919, Russia, pp. 491–92.

52. Ibid., p. 345.

53. Notes of Meeting, 20 May 1919, *FRUS*, 1919, Russia, pp. 351–53.

54. Ibid., pp. 352–53.

55. *FRUS*, 1919, Russia, p. 368.

56. De Martel to French Foreign Ministry, 4 June 1919, *FRUS*, 1919, Russia, pp. 375–78; "Reply to Admiral Kolchak," 12 June 1919, *FRUS*, 1919, Russia, p. 379; Executive Order No. 3099, 24 June 1919, *FRUS*, 1919, Russia, p. 383.

57. *FRUS*, 1919, Russia, p. 381; Grew to Polk, 25 June 1919, *FRUS*, 1919, Russia, p. 385.

58. *FRUS*, 1919, Russia, p. 424.

59. N. Gordon Levin, *Woodrow Wilson and World Politics: America's Response to War and Revolution* (New York: Oxford University Press, 1968), p. 229.

60. The Russian Political Council consisted of White Russian diplomats who lobbied the Paris Peace Conference for the right to participate at the conference as Russian regime. See Thompson, *Russia, Bolshevism, and the Versailles Peace*, pp. 66–78.

61. *PWW*, vol. 58, p. 575; *PWW*, vol. 59, p. 14; Bert E. Park, "The Impact of Wilson's Neurologic Disease During the Paris Peace Conference," *PWW*, vol. 58, p. 630; *PWW*, vol. 58, p. 367.

62. Levin, *Wilson and World Politics*, p. 232; N. Gordon Levin, "American Intervention: Aid to Liberal Russia," in Betty M. Unterberger, ed., *American Intervention in the Russian Civil War* (Lexington, Mass.: Heath, 1969), p. 107.

63. Betty M. Unterberger, "Woodrow Wilson and the Russian Revolution," in Arthur S. Link, ed., *Woodrow Wilson and a Revolutionary World* (Chapel Hill: University of North Carolina Press, 1982), p. 87.

64. As quoted in William C. Widenor, *Henry Cabot Lodge and the Search for an American Foreign Policy* (Berkeley: University of California Press, 1979), p. 316.

65. After Senator Henry Cabot Lodge criticized the peace draft on 28 February 1919, Wilson called those opposed to his plan "blind and little

provincial people . . . the littlest and most contemptible" (*PWW*, vol. 55, p. 323); Heckscher, *Woodrow Wilson*, p. 542.

66. Heckscher, *Woodrow Wilson*, pp. 595–610; Lloyd E. Ambrosius, *Woodrow Wilson and the American Diplomatic Tradition: The Treaty Fight in Perspective* (Cambridge: Cambridge University Press, 1987), p. 172; Kendrick A. Clements, *Woodrow Wilson, World Statesman* (Boston: Twayne Publishers, 1987), p. 205.

CHAPTER 5

1. Fritz T. Epstein, "Studien zur Geschichte der 'Russischen Frage' auf der Pariser Friedenskonferenz von 1919," *Jahrbücher für Geschichte Osteuropas*, N.F. 7 (1959): 456.

2. Department of State, *Papers Relating to the Foreign Relations of the United States (FRUS)*, 1920 (3 vols., Washington, D.C.: GPO, 1936), vol. 3, pp. 640–67.

3. *FRUS*, The Paris Peace Conference, 1919 (13 vols., Washington, D.C.: GPO, 1942–47), vol. 12, p. 149; Edward House, Diary, 19 September, 28 October 1918, as quoted in John M. Thompson, *Russia, Bolshevism, and the Versailles Peace* (Princeton, N.J.: Princeton University Press, 1966), p. 47.

4. Memorandum, "Notes by Professor Harper," written before 8 February 1918, Box 8, p. 1378, Charles Edward Russell Papers, Library of Congress, Washington, D.C.

5. Notes by Professor Harper, p. 1377.

6. John Spargo, *Russia as an American Problem* (New York: Harper, 1920), p. 6.

7. Ronald Radosh, "John Spargo and Wilson's Russian Policy, 1920," *Journal of American History* 52 (1965/66): 554; Spargo, *Russia as an American Problem*, p. 346.

8. Linda Killen, "The Search for a Democratic Russia: The Wilson Administration's Russian Policy, 1917–1921" (Ph.D. diss., University of North Carolina, 1975), pp. 161–65; *FRUS*, The Paris Peace Conference, vol. 12, p. 255; Department of State, Records Relating to the Internal Affairs of Russia and the Soviet Union, 1918–29. Record Group 59, Decimal File 861.00/109, National Archives, Washington, D.C.

9. Daniel M. Smith, *Aftermath of War: Bainbridge Colby and Wilsonian Diplomacy, 1920–21* (Philadelphia: American Philosophical Society, 1970), p. 74.

10. *FRUS*, 1919, Russia (Washington, D.C.: GPO, 1937), p. 130.

11. Arthur S. Link, ed., *The Papers of Woodrow Wilson (PWW)* (68 vols., Princeton, N.J.: Princeton University Press, 1966–93), vol. 63, p. 70.

12. Thompson, *Russia, Bolshevism, and the Versailles Peace*, p. 326.

13. As quoted in Thompson, *Russia, Bolshevism, and the Versailles Peace*, p. 345.

14. Adam Ulam, *Expansion and Coexistence: Soviet Foreign Policy 1917–1933* (2nd ed., New York: Holt, Rinehart and Winston, 1974), pp. 106–9.

15. Lansing to Gibson, 5 February 1920, *FRUS*, 1920, vol. 3, p. 378.

16. Smith, *Aftermath of War*, pp. 7–10.

17. Gibson to Colby, 17 July 1920, *PWW*, vol. 65, pp. 527–28; Wilson to Colby, 20 July 1920, *PWW*, vol. 65, p. 531; Wilson to Colby, 5 August 1920, *PWW*, vol. 66, p. 11. The State Department's reply criticized the Polish invasion of Russia in blunt language. Colby to Gibson, 21 August 1920, *FRUS*, 1920, vol. 3, pp. 391–92. Wilson probably did not see the State Department's reply before it was sent; see Colby to Wilson, 5 August 1920, *PWW*, vol. 66, p. 11n. 1.

18. Colby to Avezzano, 10 August 1920, *FRUS*, 1920, vol. 3, pp. 464–68.

19. *FRUS*, 1920, vol. 3, pp. 645, 651, 657.

20. Circular Note from Chicherin to Russian Representatives Abroad, 10 September 1920, Jane Degras, ed., *Soviet Documents on Foreign Policy* (3 vols., New York: Oxford University press, 1951 [Repr. Octagon, 1978]), vol. 1, p. 207.

21. *The New Republic*, 2 July 1919, p. 263; Smith, *Aftermath of War*, p. 68; Joan Hoff-Wilson, *Ideology and Economics: U.S. Relations with the Soviet Union, 1918–1933* (Columbia: University of Missouri Press, 1974), p. 18; George F. Kennan, "Russia and the Versailles Conference," *American Scholar* 30 (1960/61): 38; *FRUS*, The Paris Peace Conference, vol. 4, pp. 13–21.

22. Christopher Lasch, as quoted in Thompson, *Russia, Bolshevism, and the Versailles Peace*, p. 383.

CONCLUSIONS

1. Woodrow Wilson, "Socialism and Democracy" (22 August 1887), in Arthur S. Link, ed., *The Papers of Woodrow Wilson (PWW)* (68 vols., Princeton, N.J.: Princeton University Press, 1966–93), vol. 5, pp. 561–62.

2. Ibid., vol. 5, p. 562.

3. Woodrow Wilson, *The New Freedom* (New York: Doubleday and Page, 1913), pp. 10–11, 49–50.

4. Ibid., pp. 28, 30, 77; Samuel P. Hays, *The Response to Industrialism: 1885–1914* (Chicago: University of Chicago Press, 1957), p. 150. Throughout his life, Wilson alternated between radical statements about the severity of current social problems, as in his 1887 essay "Socialism and Democracy" (*PWW*, vol. 5, pp. 559–63) and his 1912 campaign

speeches on the one hand, and statements, such as his 1893 article on "Edmund Burke: The Man and His Times" (*PWW*, vol. 8, pp. 318–43) and his conservative social policy as exemplified by his refusal to endorse a federal child labor law after it was introduced in the House of Representatives in January 1914, on the other.

Bibliography

PRIMARY SOURCES

Unpublished Sources

National Archives, Washington, D.C.

United States Department of State. Records Relating to the Internal Affairs of Russia and the Soviet Union, 1918–29. Record Group 59, Decimal File 861.00. 861b.6363.

United States Department of State. Political Relations Between the United States and Russia and the Soviet Union, 1918–29. Record Group 59, Decimal File 711.61.

Historical Files on the American Expeditionary Force, North Russia, 1918–19. Microfilm M 924.

Library of Congress, Washington, D.C., Manuscript Division

Newton D. Baker Papers

Ray Stannard Baker Papers

Tasker H. Bliss Papers

Raymond Clapper Papers

Bainbridge Colby Papers

Josephus Daniels Papers

Robert F. Lansing Papers

William G. McAdoo Papers
John J. Pershing Papers
Elihu Root Papers
Charles Edward Russell Papers
Woodrow Wilson Papers

Published Official Documents

Browder, Robert P., and Alexander F. Kerensky. *The Russian Provisional Government 1917: Documents.* 3 vols. Stanford, Calif.: Stanford University Press, 1961.

The Bullitt Mission to Russia. Testimony of William C. Bullitt Before the Committee on Foreign Relations, United States Senate. New York: B. W. Huebsch, 1919.

Bunyan, James, ed. *Intervention, Civil War, and Communism in Russia, April–December 1918: Documents and Materials.* Baltimore: Johns Hopkins University Press, 1936 [Repr. New York: Octagon Books, 1976].

Bunyan, James, and H. H. Fisher, eds. *The Bolshevik Revolution, 1917–1918: Documents and Materials.* Stanford, Calif.: Stanford University Press, 1965.

Cockfield, Jamie H., ed. *Dollars and Diplomacy: Ambassador David Rowland Francis and the Fall of Tsarism, 1916–1917.* Durham, N.C.: Duke University Press, 1981.

Cumming, Caroline K., and Walter W. Pettit, eds. *American–Russian Relations, March 1917–March 1920: Documents and Papers.* New York: Harcourt, 1920 [Repr. Westport, Conn.: Hyperion Press, 1977].

Degras, Jane, ed. *Soviet Documents on Foreign Policy.* 3 vols. New York: Oxford University Press, 1951 [Repr: New York: Octagon, 1978].

Golder, Frank A. *Documents of Russian History, 1914–1917.* Gloucester, Mass.: P. Smith, 1964.

Hellmann, Manfred, ed. *Die russische Revolution. Von der Abdankung des Zaren bis zum Staatsstreich der Bolschewiki.* 5th ed., München: Deutscher Taschenbuch Verlag, 1984.

Lenin, Vladimir Ilich. *Collected Works.* 45 vols. Moscow: Foreign Language Publishing House, 1960–70.

McCauley, Martin, ed. *The Russian Revolution and the Soviet State 1917–1921, Documents.* London: Macmillan, 1975.

Root, Elihu. *The United States and the War: The Mission to Russia, Political Addresses.* Ed. by Robert Bacon and James B. Scott. Cambridge, Mass.: Harvard University Press, 1918.

U.S. Congress. House. Committee on Military Affairs. *American Troops in Siberia, Hearings on H[ouse] Con. Res. 30 Making Rules to Return All American Soldiers from Countries with Which We Are at Peace.* 66th Congress, 1st session, 1919. Washington, D.C.: GPO, 1919.

U.S. Congress. Senate. Committee on the Judiciary. *Bolshevik Propaganda. Hearings Before a Subcommittee on the Judiciary, United States Senate, 66th Congress, February 11, 1919 to March 10, 1919.* Washington, D.C.: GPO, 1919.

U.S. Department of State. *Papers Relating to the Foreign Relations of the United States.* 1918, Russia, 3 vols. Washington, D.C.: GPO, 1931–32.

————. 1919, Russia. Washington, D.C.: GPO. 1937.

————. 1920. 3 vols. Washington, D.C.: GPO, 1936.

————. The Paris Peace Conference, 1919. 13 vols. Washington, D.C.: GPO, 1942–47.

————. The Lansing Papers (1914–20). 2 vols. Washington, D.C.: GPO, 1940.

U.S. Department of State, *Proceedings of the Brest-Litovsk Conference: The Peace Negotiations Between Russia and the Central Powers.* Washington, D.C.: GPO, 1918.

U.S. Special Mission to Russia. *America's Message to the Russian People; Addresses by the Members of the Special Diplomatic Mission of the United States to Russia in the Year 1917.* Boston: Marshall Jones Co., 1918.

Varnock, E., and H. H. Fisher, eds. *The Testimony of Kolchak and Other Siberian Materials and Documents.* Stanford, Calif.: Stanford University Press, 1935.

Wade, Rex A., ed. *Documents of Soviet History.* Vol. 1, *The Triumph of Bolshevism, 1917–1919.* Gulf Breeze, Fla.: Academic International Press, 1991.

Zeman, Z.A.B., ed. *Germany and the Revolution in Russia, 1915–1918: Documents from the Archives of the German Foreign Ministry.* London: Oxford University Press, 1958.

Collections of Woodrow Wilson's Writings and Speeches

Baker, Ray S., ed. *Woodrow Wilson and World Settlement; Written from His Unpublished Personal Materials.* 3 vols. Garden City, N.Y.: Doubleday, 1922.

Baker, Ray S., and William E. Dodd, eds. *The Public Papers of Woodrow Wilson.* 6 vols. New York: Harper and Brothers, 1925–27.

————. *Woodrow Wilson: Life and Letters.* 8 vols. New York: Greenwood
   Press, 1927–39 [Repr. Westport, Conn.: Greenwood Press, 1968].
Link, Arthur S., ed., *The Papers of Woodrow Wilson.* 68 vols. Princeton,
   N.J.: Princeton University Press, 1966–93.
Scott, James B., ed. *President Wilson's Foreign Policy; Messages, Addresses,
   Papers,* New York: B. W. Huebsch, 1918.
Wilson, Woodrow. *The New Freedom.* New York: Doubleday and Page,
   1913.

Memoirs and Other Private Papers

Bryan, William Jennings. *The Memoirs of William Jennings Bryan.* Phila-
   delphia: John C. Winston, 1925.
Creel, George. *The War, the World and Wilson.* New York, London:
   Harper and Brothers, 1920.
————. *How We Advertised America.* New York: Arno Press, 1972.
Daniels, Josephus. *The Wilson Era: Years of War and After, 1917–23.*
   Chapel Hill: University of North Carolina Press, 1946.
Denikin, Anton I. *The Career of a Tsarist Officer: Memoirs 1872–1916.*
   Minneapolis: University of Minnesota Press, 1975.
Francis, David R. *Russia from the American Embassy, April 1916–Novem-
   ber 1918.* New York: Charles Scribner's Sons, 1921.
Graves, William S. *America's Siberian Adventure, 1918–1920.* New York:
   J. Cape and Harrison, 1931.
Hard, William. *Raymond Robins' Own Story.* New York, 1920 [Repr. New
   York: Arno Press, 1971].
Harper, Samuel N. *The Russia I Believe In.* Chicago: University of Chi-
   cago Press, 1945.
Houston, David F. *Eight Years with Wilson's Cabinet, 1913 to 1920.* 2 vols.,
   New York: Doubleday, 1926.
The Intimate Papers of Colonel House, ed. by Charles Seymour. 4 vols.
   Boston: Houghton Mifflin, 1926–28.
Kerensky, Alexander. *Prelude to Bolshevism: The Kornilov Rising.* New
   York, 1919.
————. *The Catastrophe: Kerensky's Own Story about the Russian Revolu-
   tion.* New York, London: D. Appleton and Co., 1927.
Lansing, Robert F. *The Big Four and Others of the Peace Conference.*
   Boston: Houghton Mifflin, 1921.
————. *The Peace Negotiations: A Personal Narrative.* Boston: Houghton
   Mifflin, 1921.
————. *War Memoirs of Robert Lansing, Secretary of State.* New York:
   Bobbs-Merrill, 1935.

Lloyd George, David. *War Memoirs of David Lloyd George*. London: I. Nicolson and Watson, 1933–36.

————. *Memoirs of the Peace Conference*. 2 vols. New Haven, Conn.: Yale University Press, 1939.

Miliukov, Pavel N. *Political Memoirs, 1905–1917*. Ann Arbor: University of Michigan Press, 1967.

————. *The Russian Revolution*. Ed. by Richard Stites. Gulf Breeze, Fla.: Academic International Press, 1978.

————. *Bolshevism, An International Danger*. Westport, Conn.: Hyperion Press, 1981.

Paleologue, Maurice. *An Ambassador's Memoirs*. 3 vols. London, 1923–25.

Pershing, John J. *My Experiences in the World War*. New York: Frederick A. Stokes Co., 1931.

Root, Elihu. *Russia, the American Problem. An Address*. New York: American-Russian Chamber of Commerce, 1920.

————. *Men and Policies*. Ed. by Robert Bacon and James B. Scott. Cambridge, Mass.: Harvard University Press, 1924.

Shul'gin, Vasily V. *Days of the Russian Revolution: Memoirs from the Right, 1905–1917*. Translated and edited by Bruce F. Adams. Gulf Breeze, Fla.: Academic International Press, 1990.

Sisson, Edgar. *25 November 1917–4 March 1918: One Hundred Red Days. A Personal Chronicle of the Bolshevik Revolution*. New Haven, Conn.: Yale University Press, 1931.

Journals

Literary Digest

The New Republic

New York Times

Washington Post

SECONDARY SOURCES

Books

Adelman, Jonathan R. *Prelude to the Cold War: The Tsarist, Soviet, and U.S. Armies in the Two World Wars*. Boulder and London: Lynne Rienner, 1988.

Albertson, Ralph. *Fighting Without a War: An Account of Military Intervention in North Russia*. New York: Harcourt, Brace and Howe, 1920.

Ambrosius, Lloyd E. *Woodrow Wilson and the American Diplomatic Tradition: The Treaty Fight in Perspective*. New York: Cambridge University Press, 1987.

————. *Wilsonian Statecraft: Theory and Practice of Liberal International-ism During World War I*, Wilmington, Del.: Scholarly Resources, 1991.

American Foundation, Committee on Russian American Relations, ed. *The United States and the Soviet Union. A Report on the Controlling Factors in the Relations Between the United States and the Soviet Union.* New York, 1933.

Bailey, Thomas A. *Woodrow Wilson and the Lost Peace.* New York: Macmillan, 1944 [Repr. Chicago: Quadrangle Paperbacks, 1963].

————. *Woodrow Wilson and the Great Betrayal.* New York: Macmillan, 1945.

Bell, Sidney. *Righteous Conquest. Woodrow Wilson and the Evolution of the New Diplomacy.* Port Washington, N.Y.: Kennikat Press, 1972.

Bemis, Samuel F., ed. *The American Secretaries of State and Their Diplo-macy.* Vol. X. New York: Knopf, 1929 [Repr. New York: Cooper Square Pub., 1963–].

Blum, John Morton. *Woodrow Wilson and the Politics of Morality.* Boston: Little, Brown and Co., 1956.

Bradley, John. *Allied Intervention in Russia.* London: Weidenfeld and Nicolson, 1968.

————. *Civil War in Russia 1917–1920.* New York: St. Martin's Press, 1975.

Buehrig, Edward H., ed. *Wilson's Foreign Policy in Perspective.* Bloom-ington: Indiana University Press, 1957.

————. *Woodrow Wilson and the Balance of Power.* Bloomington: Indiana University Press, 1955 [Repr. Gloucester, Mass.: P. Smith, 1968].

Bullard, Arthur. *The Russian Pendulum.* New York: Macmillan, 1919.

————. *American Diplomacy in the Modern World.* Philadelphia: Univer-sity of Pennsylvania Press, 1928.

Burdzhalov, E. N. *Russia's Second Revolution: The February 1917 Uprising in Petrograd.* Bloomington: Indiana University Press, 1987.

Calhoun, Frederick S. *Power and Principle. Armed Intervention in Wil-sonian Foreign Policy.* Kent, Ohio.: Kent State University Press, 1986.

Churchill, Winston S. *The Aftermath: The World Crisis, 1918–1928.* New York: Charles Scribner's Sons, 1929.

Clements, Kendrick A. *Woodrow Wilson, World Statesman.* Boston: Twayne Publishers, 1987.

Cooper, John M. *The Warrior and the Priest: Woodrow Wilson and Theo-dore Roosevelt.* Cambridge, Mass.: Belknap Press of Harvard University Press, 1983.

Costello, Harry J. *Why Did We Go to Russia?* Detroit: Harry J. Costello, 1920.

Daniels, Robert. *Red October: The Bolshevik Revolution of 1917.* Boston: Beacon Press, 1984.

Debo, Richard K. *Revolution and Survival: The Foreign Policy of Soviet Russia, 1917–1918.* Toronto: University of Toronto Press, 1979.

————. *Survival and Consolidation: The Foreign Policy of Soviet Russia, 1918–1941.* Montreal: McGill-Queen's University Press, 1992.

DeConde, Alexandre, ed. *Encyclopedia of American Foreign Policy.* 3 vols. New York: Charles Scribner's Sons, 1978.

Deutscher, Isaac. *The Prophet Armed: Trotsky, 1879–1921.* New York: Oxford University Press, 1954.

Devlin, Patrick. *Too Proud to Fight: Woodrow Wilson's Neutrality.* New York: Oxford University Press, 1975.

Dupuy, R. Ernest. *Perish by the Sword. The Czechoslovakian Anabasis and Our Supporting Campaigns in North Russia and Siberia 1918–1920.* Harrisburg, Pa.: Military Service Publishing Co., 1939.

Farnsworth, Beatrice. *William C. Bullitt and the Soviet Union.* Bloomington: Indiana University Press, 1967.

Ferrell, Robert H. *Woodrow Wilson and World War I, 1917–1921.* New York: Harper and Row, 1985.

Fischer, Fritz. *Germany's Aims in the First World War.* New York: W.W. Norton, 1967.

Fischer, Louis. *Russia's Road from War to Peace: Soviet Foreign Relations, 1917–1941.* New York: Harper and Row, 1969.

Florinsky, Michael T. *The End of the Russian Empire.* New York: Howard Fertig, 1973.

Floto, Inga. *Colonel House in Paris. A Study of American Policy at the Paris Peace Conference, 1919.* Princeton, N.J.: Princeton University Press, 1981.

Fowler, Wilton B. *The British–American Relations, 1917–1918: The Role of Sir William Wiseman.* Princeton, N.J.: Princeton University Press, 1969.

Frankel, Edith Ragovin, et al., eds. *Revolution in Russia: Reassessments of 1917.* New York: Cambridge University Press, 1992.

Gaddis, John Lewis. *Russia, the Soviet Union, and the United States: An Interpretive History,* New York: John Wiley and Sons, 1978.

Gardner, Lloyd C. *Wilson and Revolutions, 1913–1921.* Philadelphia: J. B. Lippincott Co., 1976.

————. *Safe for Democracy: The Anglo-American Response to Revolution, 1913–1923.* New York: Oxford University Press, 1984.

Geyer, Dietrich. *The Russian Revolution.* New York: St. Martin's Press, 1987.

Graebner, Norman, ed. *An Uncertain Tradition: American Secretaries of State in the Twentieth Century.* Westport, Conn.: Greenwood Press, 1961.

Grayson, Benson Lee, ed. *The American Image of Russia.* New York: Ungar, 1978.

————. *Russian–American Relations in World War I.* New York: Ungar, 1979.

Hahlweg, Werner. *Der Diktatfrieden von Brest-Litovsk 1918 und die bolschewistische Weltrevolution.* Münster, Westf.: Aschendorff, 1960.

Harding, Neil. *Lenin's Political Thought.* 2 vols. New York: St. Martin's Press, 1977, 1978.

Harting, Thomas Henry. *Robert Lansing: An Intimate Biography.* Ann Arbor, Mich.: 1975.

Hasegawa, Tsuyoshi, *The February Revolution: Petrograd, 1917.* Seattle: University of Washington Press, 1981.

Hays, Samuel P. *The Response to Industrialism, 1885–1914.* Chicago: University of Chicago Press, 1957.

Heckscher, August. *The Politics of Woodrow Wilson.* New York: Harper and Brothers, 1956.

————. *Woodrow Wilson.* New York: Charles Scribner's Sons, 1991.

Hellmann, Manfred, et al., eds. *Handbuch der Geschichte Russlands.* 3 vols. Stuttgart: Hiersemann, 1976–89.

Hoff-Wilson, Joan. *Ideology and Economics: U.S. Relations with the Soviet Union, 1918–1933.* Columbia: University of Missouri Press, 1974.

Hofstadter, Richard. *American Political Tradition and the Men Who Made It.* New York: Knopf, 1973.

Hoover, Herbert C. *The Ordeal of Woodrow Wilson.* New York: McGraw-Hill, 1958.

House, Edward M., and Charles F. Seymour, eds. *What Really Happened at Paris: The Story of the Peace Conference, 1918–1919.* New York: Charles Scribner's Sons, 1921.

Iriye, Akira. *The Globalizing of America, 1914–1945.* Cambridge, Mass.: Cambridge University Press, 1993.

Jessup, Philip C. *Elihu Root.* 2 vols. New York: Dodd, Mead and Co., 1938.

Kennan, George F. *Russia and the West Under Lenin and Stalin.* New York: Mentor, 1961.

————. *Soviet Foreign Policy, 1917–1941.* Huntington: R. E. Krieger and Co., 1979.

————. *The Decision to Intervene.* New York: W.W. Norton, 1984.

————. *Russia Leaves the War.* New York: W.W. Norton, 1984.

Kettle, Michael. *The Allies and the Russian Collapse, March 1917–March 1918.* London: Andre Deutsch, 1981.

————. *The Road to Intervention, March–November 1918.* London: Routledge, 1988.

————. *Churchill and the Archangel Fiasco, November 1918–July 1919.* London: Routledge, 1992.

Killen, Linda. "The Search for a Democratic Russia: The Wilson Administration's Russian Policy, 1917-1921." Ph.D. diss., University of North Carolina, 1975.

————. *The Russian Bureau: A Case Study in Wilsonian Diplomacy.* Lexington, Ky.: University of Kentucky Press, 1983.

Knock, Thomas. *To End All Wars: Woodrow Wilson and the Quest for a New World Order.* New York: Oxford University Press, 1992.

Koenig, Louis W. *Bryan: A Political Biography of William Jennings Bryan.* New York: G. P. Putnam's Sons, 1971.

Lane, David. *Politics and Society in the USSR.* New York: New York University Press, 1987.

Lasch, Christopher. "Revolution and Democracy. The Russian Revolution and the Crisis of American Liberalism." Ph.D. diss., Columbia University, 1961.

————. *The American Liberals and the Russian Revolution.* New York: McGraw-Hill, 1972.

Levin, N. Gordon. *Woodrow Wilson and World Politics: America's Response to War and Revolution.* New York: Oxford University Press, 1968.

Lincoln, W. Bruce. *Red Victory: A History of the Russian Civil War.* New York: Simon and Schuster, 1989.

————. *Passage through Armageddon: The Russians in War and Revolution, 1914-1918.* New York: Simon and Schuster, 1986.

Link, Arthur S. *Wilson.* 5 vols. Princeton, N.J.: Princeton University Press, 1947-65.

————. *Woodrow Wilson and the Progressive Era, 1910-1917.* New York: Harper and Row, 1954.

————. *Wilson the Diplomatist: A Look at His Major Foreign Policies.* Baltimore: Johns Hopkins University Press, 1957.

————. *Woodrow Wilson: A Brief Biography,* Cleveland: World Publishing Co., 1963.

————. *The Higher Realism of Woodrow Wilson and Other Essays.* Nashville, Tenn.: Vanderbilt University Press, 1971.

————, ed. *Wilson's Diplomacy: An International Symposium.* Cambridge, Mass.: Schenkman Pub. Co., 1973.

————. *Woodrow Wilson: Revolution, War, and Peace.* Arlington Heights, Ill.: Harlan Davidson Press, 1979.

————, ed. *Woodrow Wilson and a Revolutionary World, 1913-1921.* Chapel Hill: University of North Carolina Press, 1982.

Mayer, Arno J. *Wilson vs. Lenin: Political Origins of the New Diplomacy, 1917-1918.* Cleveland: Meridian, 1964.

————. *Policy and Diplomacy of Peacemaking: Containment and Counterrevolution at Versailles, 1918-1919.* New York: Knopf, 1967.

————. *Political Origins of the New Diplomacy, 1917–1918.* New York: H. Fertig, 1969.

McFadden, David W. *Alternative Path: Soviets and Americans, 1917–1920.* New York: Oxford University Press, 1993.

Nicolson, Harold. *Peacemaking 1919.* New York: Grosset and Dunlap, 1965.

Notter, Harley. *The Origins of the Foreign Policy of Woodrow Wilson.* Baltimore: Johns Hopkins University Press, 1937.

Pipes, Richard. *The Russian Revolution.* New York: Knopf, 1990.

Pope, Arthur Upham. *Maxim Litvinoff.* New York: L. B. Fischer, 1943.

Rhodes, Benjamin D. *The Anglo-American Winter War with Russia, 1918–1919: A Diplomatic and Military Tragicomedy.* New York: Greenwood, 1988.

Ruffmann, Karl-Heinz. *Sowjetrussland.* München: Deutscher Taschenbuch Verlag, 1981.

Schulte-Nordholt, Jan Willem. *Woodrow Wilson: A Life for World Peace.* Berkeley: University of California Press, 1991.

Schuman, Frederick L. *American Policy Toward Russia Since 1917. A Study of Diplomatic History, International Law and Public Opinion.* New York: International Publishers, 1928.

Seymour, Charles. *American Diplomacy During the World War.* Baltimore: Johns Hopkins University Press, 1934 [Repr. Westport, Conn.: Greenwood Press, 1975].

Shapiro, Leonard. *1917: The Russian Revolution and the Origins of Present-Day Communism.* Hounslow: Maurice Temple Smith, 1984.

Shapiro, Leonard, and Peter Reddaway, ed. *Lenin, the Man, the Theorist, the Leader. A Reappraisal.* New York: Praeger, 1967.

Silverlight, John. *The Victors' Dilemma. Allied Intervention in the Russian Civil War.* New York: Weybright and Talley, 1971.

Smith, Daniel M. *Robert Lansing and American Neutrality, 1914–1917.* Berkeley: University of California Press, 1958.

————. *The Great Departure: The United States and World War I.* New York: Knopf, 1965.

————. *Aftermath of War: Bainbridge Colby and Wilsonian Diplomacy, 1920–1921.* Philadelphia: American Philosophical Society, 1970.

Smith, Gene. *When the Cheering Stopped: The Last Years of Woodrow Wilson.* New York: Time Inc., 1966.

Spargo, John. *Sidelights on Contemporary Socialism.* New York: B. W. Huebsch, 1911.

————. *Bolshevism: The Enemy of Political and Industrial Economy.* New York, London: Harper and Brothers, 1919.

————. *The Psychology of Bolshevism.* New York: Harper, 1919.

————. *Russia as an American Problem*. New York: Harper, 1920.

Steel, Ronald. *Walter Lippmann and the American Century*. New York: Vintage, 1980.

Stewart, George. *The White Armies of Russia. A Chronicle of Counter-Revolution and Allied Intervention*. New York: Macmillan, 1933.

Stökl, Günther. *Russische Geschichte*. Stuttgart: Kröner, 1983.

Strakhovsky, Leonid I. *Intervention at Archangel. The Story of Allied Intervention and Russian Counter-Revolution in North Russia, 1918–1920*. Princeton, N.J.: Princeton University Press, 1944.

————. *American Opinion about Russia, 1917–1920*. Toronto: University of Toronto Press, 1961.

Stromberg, Roland N. *European Intellectual History Since 1789*. 4th ed. Englewood Cliffs, N.J.: Prentice-Hall, 1986.

Swettenham, John A. *Allied Intervention in Russia, 1918–1919 and the Part Played by Canada*. London: George Allen and Unwin, 1967.

Temperley, Harold William V., ed. *A History of the Peace Conference of Paris*. 6 vols. New York: Oxford University Press, 1920–24.

Thompson, John M. *Russia, Bolshevism, and the Versailles Peace*. Princeton, N.J.: Princeton University Press, 1966.

————. *Revolutionary Russia, 1917*. New York: Scribner, 1981.

Thorsen, Niels. *The Political Thought of Woodrow Wilson, 1875–1910*. Princeton, N.J.: Princeton University Press, 1988.

Tillman, Seth P. *Anglo-American Relations at the Paris Peace Conference of 1919*. Princeton, N.J.: Princeton University Press, 1961.

Ulam, Adam. *Expansion and Coexistence. Soviet Foreign Policy 1917–1933*. 2d ed., New York: Holt, Rinehart and Winston, 1974.

Ullman, Richard H. *Anglo-Soviet Relations, 1917–1921*. 3 vols. Princeton, N.J.: Princeton University Press, 1961–72.

Unterberger, Betty M. *America's Siberian Expedition, 1918–1920: A Study of National Policy*. Durham, N.C.: Duke University Press, 1956.

————, ed. *American Intervention in the Russian Civil War*. Lexington, Mass.: Heath, 1969.

————. *The United States, Revolutionary Russia, and the Rise of Czechoslovakia*. Chapel Hill: University of North Carolina Press, 1989.

Walworth, Arthur. *1918. America's Moment: American Diplomacy at the End of World War I*. New York: W.W. Norton, 1977.

————. *Woodrow Wilson*. 2 vols., 3rd ed. New York: W.W. Norton, 1978.

————. *Wilson and His Peacemakers: American Diplomacy at the Paris Peace Conference, 1919*. New York: W.W. Norton, 1986.

Warth, Robert D. *The Allies and the Russian Revolution. From the Fall of the Monarchy to the Peace of Brest-Litovsk*. New York: Russell and Russell, 1970.

Weinstein, Edwin A. *Woodrow Wilson: A Medical and Psychological Biography.* Princeton, N.J.: Princeton University Press, 1981.

Westwood, J. N. *Endurance and Endeavor: Russian History, 1812–1992.* New York: Oxford University Press, 1993.

Weyl, Walter E. *American World Policies.* Seattle: University of Washington Press, 1973.

White, John A. *The Siberian Intervention.* Princeton,N.J.: Princeton University Press, 1950.

Widenor, William C. *Henry Cabot Lodge and the Search for an American Foreign Policy.* Berkeley: University of California Press, 1979.

Wieczynski, Joseph L., ed. *Modern Encyclopedia of Russian and Soviet History.* 46 vols. Gulf Breeze, Fla.: Academic International Press, 1976–87.

Williams, William A. *American-Russian Relations, 1781–1947.* New York: Holt, Rinehart and Co., 1952.

———. *The Tragedy of American Diplomacy.* New York: Dell Publishing Co., 1962.

Wittram, Reinhard. *Studien zum Selbstverständnis des 1. und 2. Kabinetts der russischen Provisorischen Regierung, März bis Juli 1917.* Göttingen: Vandenhoeck und Ruprecht, 1971.

Articles

Epstein, Fritz T. "Zur Interpretation des Versailler Vertrages. Der von Polen 1919–1922 erhobene Reparationsanspruch." *Jahrbücher für Geschichte Osteuropas* 5 (1957): 315–35.

———. "Studien zur Geschichte der 'Russischen Frage' auf der Pariser Friedenskonferenz von 1919." *Jahrbücher für Geschichte Osteuropas* 7 (1959): 431–78.

Fike, Claude E. "The Influence of the Creel Committee and the American Red Cross on Russian-American Relations, 1917–1919." *Journal of Modern History* 31 (1959): 93–109.

———. "The United States and Russian Territorial Problems, 1917–1920." *The Historian* 24 (1962): 331–46.

Kennan, George F. "The Sisson Documents." *Journal of Modern History* 28 (1956): 130–56.

———. "American Troops in Russia." *Atlantic Monthly* 203 (1959): 36–42.

———. "Soviet Historiography and America's Role in the Intervention." *American Historical Review* 65 (1960): 302–22.

———. "Russia and the Versailles Conference." *American Scholar* 30 (1960/61): 13–42.

————. "The United States and the Soviet Union, 1917-1976." *Foreign Affairs* 54 (1976): 670-90.

Killen, Linda. "In Search for a Democratic Russia: Bakhmetev and the United States." *Diplomatic History* 2 (1978): 237-356.

Lasch, Christopher. "American Intervention in Siberia: A Reinterpretation." *Political Science Review* 77 (1962): 205-23.

Libbey, James K. "The American-Russian Chamber of Commerce." *Diplomatic History* 9 (1985): 233-48.

Long, John W. "American Intervention in Russia: The North Russian Expedition, 1918-1919." *Diplomatic History* 6 (1982): 45-67.

Radosh, Ronald. "John Spargo and Wilson's Russian Policy, 1920." *Journal of American History* 52 (1965/66): 548-65.

Rhodes, Benjamin D. "American Relief Operations at Nikolaiev, USSR, 1922-23." *The Historian* 51 (1989): 611-26.

Richard, Carl J. " 'The Shadow of a Plan.' The Rationale Behind Wilson's 1918 Siberian Intervention." *The Historian* 49 (1986): 64-84.

Richardson, W. P. "America's War in North Russia." *Current History* 13 (1921): 287-94.

Trani, Eugene P. "Woodrow Wilson and the Decision to Intervene in Russia: A Reconsideration." *Journal of Modern History* 48 (1976): 440-61.

Unterberger, Betty M. "President Wilson and the Decision to Send American Troops to Siberia." *Pacific Historical Review* 24 (1955): 63-74.

————. "The Russian Revolution and Wilson's Far Eastern Policy." *Russian Review* 16 (1957): 35-46.

————. "Woodrow Wilson and the Bolsheviks. The 'Acid Test' of Soviet-American Relations." *Diplomatic History* 11 (1987): 71-90.

Weinstein, Edwin A. "Woodrow Wilson's Neurological Illness." *Journal of American History* (1970): 324-51.

Index

About the Author

GEORG SCHILD is Wissenschaftlicher Mitarbeiter in the Department of Political Science and Contemporary History at the University of Bonn. He received his Ph.D. from the University of Maryland at College Park and is the Author of *Bretton Woods and Dumbarton Oaks*, 1995.

ISBN 0-313-29570-0

EAN

9 780313 295706

HARDCOVER BAR CODE